MESSERSCHMITT Bf 109

THE LATTER YEARS – WAR IN THE EAST TO THE FALL OF GERMANY

AIR WAR ARCHIVE

MESSERSCHMITT Bf 109

THE LATTER YEARS – WAR IN THE EAST TO THE FALL OF GERMANY

CHRIS GOSS

FRONTLINE
BOOKS

MESSERSCHMITT Bf 109
The Latter Years – War in the East to the Fall of Germany

This edition published in 2019 by Frontline Books,
an imprint of Frontline Books,
47 Church Street, Barnsley, S. Yorkshire, S70 2AS

ISBN: 978-1-47389-948-3

CIP data records for this title are available from the British Library

For more information on our books, please visit
www.frontline-books.com,
email info@frontline-books.com
or write to us at the above address.

Typeset by Aura Technology and Software Services, India
Printed and bound by CPI Group (UK) Ltd, Croydon, CR0 4YY

Typeset in 9.5/12pt Avenir

CONTENTS

PREFACE

My Air War Archive book on the Focke-Wulf Fw 190 published in 2019 explained how I obtained many photos from the eminent aviation historian and writer, the late Dr Alfred Price. Having already written the Air War Archive book *Messerschmitt Bf 109: The Early Years* (2018), I was concerned that I had insufficient photographs for a second volume covering the years 1941 to 1945. However, I have looked closely at what I had in my collection as well as what Alfred gifted me and, yet again encouraged (cajoled?) by Martin Mace of Frontline Books, I have been able to produce a second book of his and my photos covering the later versions of the Bf 109 with as full captions as possible illustrating this famous fighter. Again, this and other books in the series are not intended to be an in-depth study of the aircraft and its operational history as there are many others out there who are far better qualified to do this. Rather it recognizes the work done by the late Brian Philpott in his World War 2 Photo Album series published by Patrick Stephens in the late 1970s and aims to give the reader as much information as possible on the photo in question.

Chris Goss, Marlow, 2019

ACKNOWLEDGEMENTS

First and foremost the late Dr Alfred Price for his generosity and advice and the late Bryan Philpott for inspiration. In no particular order of thanks: Franck Benoiton (Italy), Maciej Goralczyk (Poland), the late Manfred Griehl (Germany), Eggert Norâdahl (Iceland), Tim Oliver (UK), the late Michael Payne (UK), Geoff Rayner (UK), Bernd Rauchbach (Germany), Matti Salonen (Finland), Andy Thomas (UK) and Dave Wadman (Canada)

INTRODUCTION: THE CAPTURE OF THE FIRST BF 109 F

Rolf Peter Pingel was born in Kiel on 1 October 1913 and when old enough, joined the Luftwaffe. On completion of his training, he was posted to I./JG 134 at Wiesbaden-Erbenheim in March 1937. During the Spanish Civil War, he flew with 2.J/88, shooting down six aircraft for which he was awarded the Spanish Cross in Gold with Swords. On his return to Germany at the end of 1937, he was given command of 2./JG 334 which was eventually re-designated 2./JG 53.

Pingel's first kill of the Second World War was a French Mureaux 113 of GAO 1/506 on 10 September 1939, followed by a Fairey Battle of 150 Squadron on 30 September. His next kill was not until 14 May 1940 when he shot down three French and one British aircraft in a single day. By the end of the Battle of France, he had shot down eight aircraft (the last two when he was acting as Gruppen Kommandeur of III./JG 53 following the shooting down and capture of his good friend Werner Mölders on 5 June 1940). Returning to 2./JG 53 for the Battle of Britain, Hauptmann Pingel shot down two more RAF aircraft before he was posted to command I./JG 26 on 22 August 1940 when command of JG 26 was given to Major Adolf Galland.

Pingel would be awarded the Ritterkreuz on 14 September 1940 and by 28 September 1940 had shot down a total of twenty-two aircraft. However, his kill of 28 September 1940 (a Hurricane near Maidstone believed to be flown by Pilot Officer Albert Lewis of 249 Squadron) would be his last of the Battle of Britain. Pingel recalls what happened on the afternoon of 28 September 1940 as follows:

> I was followed by a fighter to a place about 10 miles north-west of Boulogne where I force-landed in the sea. Shortly before I landed, the British pilot drew alongside, opened his canopy, shook his head and turned back for England. I had been shot by hundreds of bullets, the engine did not work. I tried to escape through the clouds but whenever I reappeared on the other side, the British fighter was again behind me. My armour plating behind my head saved my life.

Slightly injured, Pingel was quickly picked up by the German air-sea rescue service.

Confusion has arisen about this combat. Recent research, reinforced by Pingel's own account, confirms that it was in the Channel off Boulogne (not off the Isle of Wight when he was still with 2./ JG 53) and that the ditching was shortly after his kill timed at 1440hrs (German time). It has been suggested that his nemesis was Sergeant John Beard of 249 Squadron but even though Beard's combat report almost matches, the time was three hours before Pingel's combat near Maidstone. It was more likely that Beard shot down Feldwebel Fritz Schür of 3./JG 26, the only other Bf 109 lost that day, which was apparently shot down in the morning off Dover. The only other RAF pilot that claimed a Bf 109 at the time Pingel made his claim was Pilot Officer Ben Bennions of 41 Squadron who claimed two Bf 109 probables during a high-altitude combat between Canterbury and Newhaven at 1340hrs (UK time). Seven Spitfires were attacked by Bf 109s at 27,000ft and two returned badly damaged, one being flown by Bennions himself. He was '. . . knocking bits off a 109 . . .' when he came under attack himself after which he claimed another 109 probable 'four miles south of Brighton'. It is therefore more likely to assume that he shot down Pingel.

Pingel would shoot down one more RAF fighter before the end of the year (a Spitfire near Gravesend on 5 November 1940) but his next kill was not until 16 June 1941 (a Blenheim of 59 Squadron). By 2 July 1941, he had shot down a total of twenty-eight aircraft in Spain and over north-west Europe but he would shoot down nothing further as in retrospect he perhaps tried a little too hard on 10 July 1941 to increase his score.

The target for Circus 42 on 10 July 1941 was Chocques Power Station, north-west of Béthune in northern France. Three Stirlings of 7 Squadron, flown by Pilot Officer Dennis Witts, Pilot Officer Charles Rolfe and Pilot Officer Cecil Fraser DFC, lifted off from Oakington in Cambridgeshire at 1030hrs, each laden with five 1,000lb and ten 500lb bombs. The escort was massive but from Fighter Command's perspective, Circus 42 was not that successful, as illustrated by the Biggin Hill Wing's participation.

Thirty-three Spitfires lead by Squadron Leader Michael Robinson of 609 Squadron were tasked to be close escort for the three Stirlings. They were briefed to reach the French coast two minutes ahead of the bombers, sweep the coast between Hardelot and Le Touquet, re-join the bombers to the target and then break away, sweeping back between Gravelines and Calais.

Shortly after take-off, one of the Biggin Hill squadrons was re-tasked to intercept an enemy raid which turned out to be friendly and then the CO of 92 Squadron, Squadron Leader Jamie Rankin, broke away as his engine was overheating. Due to the need to maintain radio silence, he was unable to say that he was landing at Hawkinge and two sections blindly followed him down, although one didn't land.

Even before the Stirlings crossed the French coast, disaster struck. Approaching Boulogne and its Flak defences, serial N6017 flown by Pilot Officer Cecil Fraser DFC received a very accurate salvo of four bursts and suffered a direct hit. The massive bomber rolled onto its back and dived into the sea five miles south of Hardelot; three crew were seen to bale out but there were no survivors from its crew of seven. Cecil Fraser's body was later washed ashore in Holland, one crew member is still listed as missing and the remainder were buried in Boulogne. Canadian Cecil Fraser had already flown a tour on Wellingtons with 115 Squadron for which he was awarded the DFC, his citation reading:

> This officer was detailed to attack an aerodrome near Munster. Adverse weather conditions made it necessary for Pilot Officer Fraser to dive to a low altitude. In doing so one engine failed but undeterred he continued his run and dropped his bombs, putting a stick across the target and hitting the watch office. By coolness and skill he made a successful recovery. On another occasion he brought his aircraft back from

his target in the Ruhr on one engine. During another raid he succeeded in reaching commencement of the and successfully bombing his target after a running fight with a Messerschmitt 110. Since the war this officer has taken part in one sweep and 28 major operations. The quite exceptional keenness and unconcerned gallantry displayed by Pilot Officer Fraser are worthy of the highest traditions of the Service.

Cecil Fraser died nine days short of his 23rd birthday.

South of Boulogne, the first German fighters were seen and both the RAF and Luftwaffe pilots started circling to get the best position to attack. However, German aircraft began splitting away. Michael Robinson managed to follow a Bf 109 in a steep dive which poured black smoke after being hit and 30 miles inland from Le Touquet, the German fighter's wings then broke off. Flight Lieutenant Paul Richey also reported damaging a Bf 109 but who shot down who over France is confused – RAF fighters claimed eleven destroyed, two probables and three damaged but the Germans only lost three fighters destroyed and one damaged.

For the British fighters, losses were much heavier. Two of the 92 Squadron Spitfires which landed at Hawkinge took off and were immediately vectored towards fifteen Bf 109s which promptly bounced them. Sergeant Gordon Waldern dived, weaving all the time, but when he was eight miles north of Manston, a cannon shell exploded in his cockpit, blowing away the control column and damaging the glycol tank. With difficulty he baled out and was rescued after nearly five hours in his dinghy (Waldern rejoined his squadron four days later but was then shot down and killed on 19 July 1941).

72 Squadron lost contact with the rest of the Wing, and circled to try and rejoin only to be comprehensively bounced (two from above port, another two above starboard and four from below and port) by Bf 109s over Fruges. Heading for a fog bank, on emerging two Spitfires (flown by Flying Officer Jerzy Godlewski and Sergeant Allan Casey) were seen to be missing and then Squadron Leader Desmond Sheen saw who he thought was Sergeant Charles Harrison being attacked and his Spitfire dive into the ground without the pilot baling out (in 2004, Harrison's identity tag was found on the beach at Nieuport in Belgium which would indicate that he had in fact crashed into the sea). To make matters worse, on heading for home, 72 Squadron got lost in fog and landfall was made north of the Thames so instead of landing at Biggin Hill in Kent, they landed at Coltishall in Norfolk, the Spitfire of Sergeant Jim Rosser crash-landing when his engine cut out.

In total, 72 Squadron suffered three pilots killed (Harrison, Casey and Godlewski), 92 Squadron lost one (Waldern), 610 Squadron had two pilots captured (Pilot Officer Peter Ward-Smith and Sergeant John Anderson) and one killed (Sergeant Horace Blackman) and 611 Squadron one killed (Sergeant Leslie Hemmingway) – most of these fell into the Channel. Claims for eight Spitfires were filed by JG 2 and another two by JG 26.

In all this confusion, the remaining two Stirlings bombed their target and turned for home. Twelve Hurricanes of 306 Squadron were now tasked as rear cover together with two other squadrons and to meet the Stirlings but as the bombers approached, it was clear that they were not alone. 306 Squadron, flying at 2,000ft, initially reported nothing except light Flak in the Calais area as the Stirlings crossed the coast. Heading back for Dover at 1,500ft, Sergeant Jan Smigielski saw four unidentified aircraft behind him and shouted a warning. It was then he spotted a German aircraft below him.

In Stirling W7433 captained by Pilot Officer Charles Rolfe, they reported successfully bombing the target on a course 70° across target and then turned for home. They then reported that they were attacked by a single Me 109 and received hits in the tail by cannon fire. However, the beam gunner (the identity of whom is hard to ascertain) reported hitting this aircraft in the engine and claimed it as damaged. The Stirling landed back at Oakington at 1330hrs

This almost matches with what Rolf Pingel reported. He followed a Stirling, an aircraft he described as '. . . a formidable opponent even for a fighter as it was well able to look after itself . . . pouring cannon fire from every orifice'. However, according to him he did not open fire and then lost the aircraft in haze. No other German pilot from either JG 2 or JG 26 makes any mention of attacking a Stirling so it must be assumed that Pingel did attack Charles Rolfe's Stirling, causing the damage.

However, Sergeant Smigielski (whose combat report no longer exists even if one was filed) is reported to have attacked a lone Bf 109 which must have been flying at around 1,000ft which crashed in a field near South Foreland. Another report says 'An Me 109 was chased and fired at and it was originally claimed as destroyed as it made a crash-landing near Dover'. However, the first report then states 'Not allowed. E/a landed thru engine trouble' whilst the second states '. . . investigation proved it had not been hit'.

Pingel stated that his engine failed and that he did not know whether the Stirling or some Spitfires [sic], which he had seen, had attacked him or not. He did acknowledge seeing Hurricanes (which were escorting a Lysander, presumably from Hawkinge's Air-Sea Rescue Flight) which then circled him before flying away. The fact that Pingel was seen at around 1,000ft would indicate that something was wrong with his aircraft – the Stirlings would not have been flying that low over the Channel so problems must have occurred after Pingel's attack on Charles Rolfe's bomber.

The final piece of the jigsaw is the technical evaluation of Pingel's belly-landed Bf 109 F-2 which was described as being in very good condition. The report dated 11 July 1941 stated: 'It is reported that this aircraft was in action with fighters, but no bullet strikes have yet been found in the airframe or engine. The pilot made a good belly landing and the machine is in good condition. It is possible that there was engine failure.' It is clear from photos taken after the crash that the engine had stopped and the propeller was gently windmilling, hence two blades and just the tip of the third were bent back.

Over the following weeks and months the Royal Aircraft Establishment raised a series of very detailed reports on Pingel's Bf 109 F-2, an aircraft which had only recently entered operational service in significant numbers and did suffer from a number of technical problems. No mention is made of any combat damage or cause for loss but it did analyse the engine and coolant system in some detail, a final comment in the report being: 'The coolant header tanks on either side of the engine are very vulnerable to shots from either quarter.'

It is therefore safe to assume that Pingel was not shot down – the lack of bullet damage, no combat reports for both 7 or 306 Squadrons and the statements that the claims had been withdrawn due to lack of bullet damage being proof of this. It looks like bad luck caused his demise, the RAF only being indirectly responsible. Rolf Pingel would pass away on 4 April 2000.

BASIC BF 109 OPERATIONAL VARIANTS 1941–1945

Variant	Engine	Basic Armament	Other Changes
E-7	DB601A or N	2 x 7.92mm MG 17, 2 x 20mm MG FF/M	Fitted with 300-litre drop tank
T-1	DB 601N	"	Intended for used on *Graf Zeppelin* carrier
T-2	"	"	As T-1 but carrier equipment removed
F-1	"	2 x 7.92mm MG 17, 1 x 20mm MG FF/M	

F-2	"	2 x 7.92mm MG 17, 1 x 15mm MG 151/15	
F-4	DB 601E	2 x 7.92mm MG 17, 1 x 20mm MG 151/20	
G-1	DB605A	2 x 7.92mm MG 17, 1 x 20mm MG 151/20; possible 2 x underwing 20mm MG 151/20	Pressurized cockpit
G-2	"	"	
G-3	"	"	As G-1 but new radio
G-4	"	"	As G-2 but new radio
G-5	"	2 x 13mm MG 131, 1 x 20mm MG 151/20	Pressurized cockpit
G-6	"	2 x 13mm MG 131, 1 x 20mm x MG 151/20; possible underwing 21cm rockets instead of MG 151/20	
G-8	'	2 x 13mm MG 131	Recce
G-10	DB 605D	2 x 13mm MG 131, 1 x 20mm MG 151/20 or 30mm MK 108	
G-12	DB 605A	2 x 7.92mm MG 17	Two-seat trainer
G-14	DB 605AM	2 x 13mm MG 131, 1 x 20mm MG 151/20	
K-4	DB 605D	2 x 13mm MG 131/15mm MG 151/15, 1 x 30mm MK 103/108	
K-14	DB 605L	2 x 13mm MG 131, 1 x 30mm MK 108	Very limited numbers, if any, went operational

Hauptmann Rolf Pingel, formerly Staffelkapitän of 2./JG 53 and then Gruppen Kommandeur of I./JG 26. He was awarded the Ritterkreuz on 14 September 1940.

At 1340hrs on 10 July 1941, Rolf Pingel's Bf 109 F-2, Wk Nr 12764 coded <<+, force-landed at St Margaret's Bay, Dover, Kent. Any attempt by Pingel to set fire to his aircraft was apparently prevented by a burst of gunfire over his head.

The RAF was quick to recover this aircraft, the condition of which was good despite the forced landing. Its camouflage was described as dark olive-green upper surfaces and pale blue underneath. The rudder was yellow with twenty-two victory bars. It appears that the spinner was half-white half-black. A plate on the fin was inscribed 'Arado Flugzeug Werke 1941 Wk Nr 889' whilst the main plate on the fuselage said it was built by AGO Flugzeug Werke Ochersleben 1941.

Now at the Royal Aircraft Establishment (RAE), Farnborough, the undercarriage was lowered. The only visible damage appears to be the propeller. Note the maker's plate on the nose behind the spinner.

Above: Another view taken at St Margaret's Bay shows the spinner colours and the black edged in white Gruppen Kommandeur's chevrons.

Right: Pingel had no time to jettison his canopy. Note the oxygen-charging point and behind it a 24-volt socket.

The cowling has been removed showing the engine bearer and two guns on top of the engine.

The view from the port side shows clearly the stencilling, fuel triangle, first aid kit access and the twenty-two victory bars.

The tail also shows in detail more stencilling and the Arado plate. The aircraft was repaired, given the serial ES906 and first flew again on 19 September 1941 after which it was delivered to the Air Fighting Development Unit at RAF Duxford. It was then lost in an accident when it crashed at Fowlmere, Cambridgeshire, on 20 October 1941, killing its pilot, Flying Officer Marian Skalski. Pingel was forced to land due to probable engine trouble; Skalski was apparently overcome by carbon monoxide.

GLOSSARY AND ABBREVIATIONS

Adj	Adjutant
Aufklärer	Reconnaissance
Bf	Bayerische Flugzeugwerke (Prefix for Messerschmitt Bf 109 and 110)
Brillanten	Knight's Cross with Oak Leaves, Swords and Diamonds
Deckungsrotte	Lookout pair
Deutsches Kreuz in Gold	German Cross in Gold
E/A	Enemy aircraft
EAC	Enemy Aircraft Flight
Ehrenpokal (Pokal)	Goblet of Honour – awarded for outstanding achievements in the air war
Eiserne Kreuz	Iron Cross (came in First and Second Class)
Ergänzungs (Erg)	Training
Erprobungsgruppe	Experimental Wing
Experte	Ace
Fähnrich/Oberfähnrich	Officer Cadet/Senior Officer Cadet
Feindflug	Operational flight
Feldwebel	Flight Sergeant
Flak	Anti-aircraft
Fluzeugführer (F)	Pilot
Freie Jagd	Free hunting fighter sweep
Führer	Leader
Gefreiter (Gefr)	Leading Aircraftman
Generalfeldmarschall	Air Chief Marshal
Geschwader (Gesch)	Group consisting three Gruppen commanded by a Geschwader Kommodore
Gruppe (Gr) Kommandeur. Gruppe number	Wing consisting three Staffeln; commanded by a Gruppen denoted by Roman numerals (e.g. II).
Hauptmann	Flight Lieutenant/Captain
Holzauge	Lookout
Ia	Operations Officer

Jabo	Fighter-bomber
Jagd	Fighter
Jagdfliegerschule (JFS)	Fighter pilot school
Jagdgeschwader (JG)	Fighter Group
Jagdgruppe (JGr)	Fighter Wing
Kampfgeschwader (KG)	Bomber Group
Kette	Three-aircraft tactical formation similar to RAF vic
Leutnant	Pilot Officer/2nd Lieutenant
Lehrer	Instructor
Luftflotte	Air Fleet
Major	Squadron Leader/Major
Nachtrichtenoffizier (NO)	Communications Officer
Nahaufklärungsgruppe (NAG)	Short-range reconnaissance Wing (NAG)
Oberfeldwebel	Warrant Officer
Obergefreiter	Senior Aircraftman/Corporal
Oberleutnant	Flying Officer/1st Lieutenant
Oberst	Group Captain/Colonel
Oberstleutnant	Wing Commander/Lieutenant-Colonel
Reichsluftfahrtministerium	Air Ministry
Reichsmarschall	Marshal of the Air Force
Ritterkreuz	Knight's Cross
Ritterkreuz mit Eichenlaub	Knight's Cross with Oak Leaves
Rotte	Two-aircraft tactical formation; two Rotten made a Schwarm; commanded by a Rottenführer
Rottenflieger	Wingman
SAAF	South African Air Force
Schlacht (S)	Ground attack
Schnell	Fast
Schwarm	Four-aircraft tactical formation commanded by a Schwarm Führer
Schwerter	Knight's Cross with Oak Leaves and Swords
Seenot	Air Sea Rescue
Sonderstaffel	Special Staffel
Stab	Staff or HQ; formation in which Gruppen Kommandeur and Geschwader Kommodore flew
Stabsfeldwebel	Senior Warrant Officer
Staffel (St)	Squadron (12 aircraft); commanded by a Staffel Kapitän. Staffel number denoted by Arabic numerals (e,g.2)
Technischer Offizier (TO)	Technical Officer
Unteroffizier	Sergeant
Werk Nummer (Wk Nr)	Serial Number
Zerstörer (Z)	Destroyer/Heavy fighter
Zerstörergeschwader (ZG)	Heavy Fighter Group

1941

Geschwader Kommodore of JG 51 Major Werner Mölders' Bf 109 F seen at Pihen, late 1940/early 1941. Bf 109 F-1 Wk Nr 5628 and carrying the factory code SG+GW on the fuselage arrived at Pihen, south-west of Calais, in early October 1940. The fuselage was repainted with Geschwader Kommodore's chevrons and the nose and rudder painted yellow. Mölders first flew this aircraft on an operational flight on 7 October 1940 but from 10 to 17 October, went back to flying his Bf 109 E-4/N. During this time he increased his score to forty-eight. However, at 1403hrs UK time on 22 October 1940, he lifted off from Pihen and 45 minutes later recorded the first kills of the war for a Bf 109 F.

An F-2 Wk Nr 6060 arrived for Mölders to fly at the end of January 1941. This aircraft has 65 kill markings on its rudder, the 65th being a Hurricane south-west of Dungeness at 1842hrs on 16 April 1941. His victim was possibly either Squadron Leader John O'Neil CO of 601 Squadron, Wing Commander Graham Manton, the RAF Northolt Wing Leader, or Group Captain Theodore McEvoy, RAF Northolt Station Commander, all three being slightly wounded. Hermann-Friedrich Joppien of Stab I./JG 51, Leutnant Heinz Bär of 1./JG 51 and Leutnant Georg Seelmann of 11./JG 51 also claimed Hurricanes in the Dungeness/Lydd area.

Mölders with pilots of JG 51, Mardyck, 1941. Second from right is Feldwebel Erwin Fleig of 1./JG 51. By the time JG 51 had left the Channel coast in May 1941, Fleig had shot down nine aircraft. He would be awarded the Ritterkreuz on 12 August 1941, would be commissioned and then given command of 2./JG 51 in April 1942. However, on 29 May 1942, he was shot down in combat with Soviet fighters flying a Bf 109 F-2 Wk Nr 9802 and was captured. His score at that time was sixty-six aircraft, all but nine being in the East.

Opposite: Werner Mölders in the cockpit of his Bf 109 F-2, early 1941. Not the distinctive larger air intake compared to the Bf 109 E.

Mölders posing with ground crew, Mardyck, April 1941. It would appear that the JG 51 eagle's head is painted both sides of the yellow cowling.

Oberleutnant Hans Ohly, Staffelkapitän of 1./JG 53. Ohly had flown with 1./JG 53 in the Battle of France and Battle of Britain, getting his fourth kill on 26 August 1940. He took command of 1./JG 53 at the start of September 1940. On 19 December 1940, 1./JG 53 returned to Krefeld and then at Mannheim on 15 March 1941 Ohly first flew the Bf 109 F. He returned to the Channel front on 2 April 1941 and flew his first operational flight in White 7 from Crécy on 4 April 1941 and then flew another thirty-two, mainly in this aircraft, before moving east on 23 May 1941. He would survive the war.

Hans Ohly in Bf 109 F-2 White 7, Crécy, April 1941. Note the spinner and cowling are yellow.

Bf 109 Fs of III./JG 2 photographed at Roquancourt, spring 1941.

This Bf 109 E-7 was photographed by the crew of a Ju 88 of 1 Staffel (Fern)./Aufklärungsgruppe 120 which in 1941 was based at Stavanger in Norway. The lack of a unit badge and markings possibly makes this an aircraft of 4 (Einsätz)/JGr Drontheim which operated from Trondheim from 19 April 1941 flying a mix of Bf 109s and Bf 109 T-2s, the latter being aircraft intended for use on the carrier *Graf Zeppelin*. Also at Stavanger was I./JG 77.

Seen at Belgrad-Semlin in May 1941 are Bf 109 Es of Hauptmann Dietrich Hrabak's II./JG 54 and Major Alexander von Winterfeldt's III./JG 77. II./JG 54 is in the process of converting to the Bf 109 F-2 and III./JG 77 are receiving the older Bf 109 Es. Note the distinctive camouflage on the White 2 of Oberleutnant Hans Philipp's 4./JG 54, the Lion of Aspern badge and the yellow rudder and cowling. Both units had recently taken part in the Balkan campaign.

This Bf 109 F has very dark camouflage after what appears to be a black spinner and yellow cowling. The lack of any fuselage band would indicate this to be either JG 2 or JG 26.

Pilots of III./JG 2, Roquancourt, spring 1941. Unteroffizier Rudi Rothenfelder (9./JG 2), ?, and Leutnant Christian von Schlieffen (7./JG 2). Von Schilieffen was shot down and killed in combat on 25 June 1941 flying Bf 109 F-2 Wk Nr 12709, which crashed near Wirwignes in the Pas de Calais. He claimed his only kill, a Spitfire, on the same day at 1258hrs.

Pilots of III./JG 2 at readiness, Roquancourt, spring 1941; only one of them would survive the war. Leutnant Martin Adolph (9./JG 2, killed in action 22 June 1941), Feldwebel Hans Jahner (9./JG 2, wounded 2 July 1941), Unteroffizier Johann Straub (9./JG 2, killed in action 23 June 1941), Oberleutnant Werner Stöckelmann (Stab III./JG 2, killed in an accident 29 May 1942) and Unteroffizier Karl Nowak (9./JG 2, killed in action 10 June 1942).

Armourers of III./JG 2 preparing belted 7.92mm ammunition for the Bf 109 F-2's MG 17 machine guns, Roquancourt, spring 1941.

Feldwebel Heinz Jahner of 9./JG 2 getting into his Bf 109 F-2, Roquancourt, spring 1941.

Oberleutnant Bruno Stolle, Staffelkapitän of 8./JG 2 since the start of September 1940, alongside his Bf 109 F-2 Black 11+I. For much of 1941, III./JG 2 was based at St Pol Brias. Stolle would end 1941 on a high, shooting down two Spitfires of 234 Squadron flown by Pilot Officer Frank Clarke and Sergeant John Walker who were engaged on a shipping recce in the Channel. These were his 14th and 15th victories. Both RAF pilots were killed. III./JG 2 converted to the Fw 190 in June 1942.

Right: Combat damage to Feldwebel Heinz Jahner's Bf 109 F-2 Yellow 8+I of 9./ JG 2, 23 June 1941. It would appear that his aircraft has been damaged by two 20mm rounds, the splinter damage evident on the starboard side of the fuselage. A number of claims for aircraft damaged that day were filed by the RAF.

Below: The entry holes on Yellow 8+I neatly bracketing either side of the fuselage cross.

Jahner's Bf 109 F-2 also suffered damage to the starboard aileron.

Heinz Jahner next to an undamaged Yellow 8+I. Jahner had begun the war flying the Fw 189 with 9 (Heer)./Lehrgeschwader 2 and converted to the Bf 109 during the Battle of Britain.

Heinz Jahner and Feldwebel Karl 'Buck' Nowak of 9./JG 2 standing next to what could be Nowak's Bf 109 F-2. Nowak's first kill was a Blenheim on 4 July 1941, the only one lost that day being one from 226 Squadron which crashed near Dunkirk. There are five kill bars on the rudder of this aircraft, Nowak's fifth kill being a Whirlwind on 4 September 1941. He would end the year with seven kills but would be killed in combat with 41 Squadron on 10 June 1942, his Fw 190 crashing off the Isle of Wight. By the time of his death he had claimed to have shot down twelve aircraft.

A Bf 109 F of JG 26 coming into land, 1941. The lack of any markings behind the fuselage cross would indicate I Gruppe which was commanded by Hauptmann Rolf Pingel until 10 July 1941 and then Hauptmann Johannes Seifert. I./JG 26 began converting from the Bf 109 E-7 to the Bf 109 F-2 in July 1941. This photo was probably taken at St Omer-Clairmarais.

A publicity photo of an unidentified pilot from III./JG 2 at St Pol-Brias. The Hahnkopf (cockerel's head) emblem was adopted following Hauptmann Hans 'Assi' Hahn becoming the Gruppen Kommandeur.

It was not uncommon for the Ergänzungsgruppe of the various fighter Geschwader to get involved in combat in 1941. For most of 1941, Erg.Gr./JG 53, was commanded by Hauptmann Hubert Kroeck. 1 Staffel was based at Vannes-Meucon and 2 Staffel St Jean D'Angely and La Rochelle. Second from the right is Oberfeldwebel Franz Gawlik of 2 Staffel and formerly of 2./JG 53. On 24 July 1941, he and five other pilots of his Staffel claimed to have shot down Halifaxes from 35 and 76 Squadrons attacking La Pallice.

In February 1941, I./JG 77, also known as Jagdgruppe Stavanger, was formed, commanded by Hauptmann Walter Grommes, former Staffelkapitän of 5./ZG 76, flying the Bf 109 E-4, E-7 and T-2. The previous I./JG 77 had moved to France in August 1940 and became IV./JG 51. Stab I was based at Stavanger-Sola, 1./JG 77 at Mandal, 2./JG 77 at Lister and 3./JG 77 at Herdla. This photograph was taken in spring 1941.

The Stabschwarm of JG 2, St Pol-Brias, 1 August 1941, on the award of the Ritterkreuz to two of them. Oberleutnant Erich Leie (twenty-one kills as of this date, Ritterkreuz 1 August 1941, killed in action 7 March 1945), Major Walter Oesau (eighty-six kills as of this date, Schwerter 15 July 1941, killed in action 11 May 1944), Oberleutnant Rudi Pflanz (nineteen kills as of this date, Ritterkreuz 1 August 1941, killed in action 31 July 1942), and Feldwebel Günther Seeger (twelve kills as of this date, Ritterkreuz 26 March 1944).

A Bf 109 F of I./JG 26 is pushed to where no doubt the damage to its port aileron can be repaired, St Omer-Clairmarais, summer 1941.

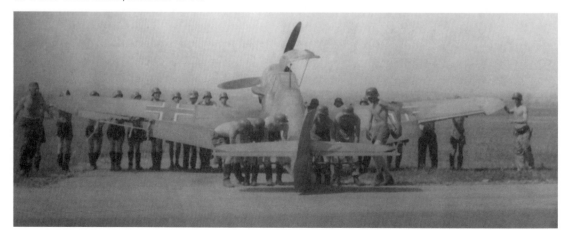

Left: Forty kills on the rudder of Oberleutnant Josef Priller's Bf 109 F-2 White 1 of 1./JG 26, St Omer-Clairmarais. Priller shot down his 40th aircraft, a Spitfire of 72 Squadron flown by Sergeant Bill Lamberton, on 14 July 1941; his next came five days later so this dates the photograph fairly well.

Below: A profile view of Priller's F-2 White 1. The rudder is yellow and the spinner black. Priller's personal badge, a playing card with the ace of hearts, is the light patch on the fuselage below the front of the cockpit. There appears to be no other badge on this aircraft.

Hit by return fire from the Wellington he was attacking, Leutnant Julius Meimberg, Staffelkapitän of 3./JG 2, force-landed his Bf 109 E-7, Wk Nr 7671 Yellow 1, at Brélès, 7.5km north-east of St Renan in Brittany at 1512hrs on 24 July 1941. There are eleven kill markings on the rudder, his 11th being a Spitfire, probably from 234 Squadron flown by Sergeant R. T. Martin, shot down near Etaples on 17 July 1941. The injured German pilot is lying on the ground being attended to.

Meimberg's Yellow 1 (the number is just visible) shows how it has skidded into a bank; the middle of the canopy has been jettisoned.

Believed to be Bf 109 E-4s of Erg./JG 26, early 1941. It is thought that this photo was taken at Cazaux in south-western France but this unit, commanded initially by Oberleutnant Hubertus von Holtey (formerly of 5./JG 26) but when it became a Gruppe commanded by Hauptmann Fritz Fromme, a former First World War fighter pilot, was based at Cognac.

The Bf 109 F of Major Adolf Galland, Kommodore of JG 26, with sixty-nine victory bars. His 69th was a Blenheim of 226 Squadron on 2 July 1941, and the 70th came on 23 July 1941. The photograph was possible taken at Audembert or Clairmarais between those two dates.

A radio mechanic working on a Bf 109 F-2 of III./JG 2, Roquancourt, 1941.

Feldwebel Heinz Jahner of 9./JG 2 together with a Messerschmitt engineer, Antwerp, early 1941. It is believed that Jahner is collecting a new aircraft. Note the apparent lack of a gun sight.

Heinz Jahner posing on the yellow cowling of a Bf 109 F-2. Note the spray-painted 9 Staffel mosquito badge and the engine starter handle.

Unteroffizier Johann Straub on the cowling of another 9./JG 2 Bf 109 F-2. Note the aircraft's Wk Nr is painted on the handle. Twenty-year-old Austrian Straub was flying Wk Nr 5763 when he was shot down north-west of St Omer on 23 June 1941, dying of his injures in the hospital at St Omer the same day. He would have been 21 sixteen days later.

Bf 109 F-2 Yellow 6 of 9./JG 2 framed through the undercarriage of another Bf 109 F of III./JG 2, Roquancourt, summer 1941.

Leutnant Martin Adolph, Unteroffizier Karl Nowak and Unteroffizier Johann Straub of 9./JG 2, Roquancourt, May–June 1941. Adolph would be killed in action on 22 June 1941, and Straub a day after that whilst Nowak would survive almost another year.

Yellow 6 presumed to be from 9./JG 2 (although no vertical bar can be seen on it or on Yellow 11 behind it) with the tail of one of the Geschwader's victims, early summer 1941. Note the absence of a yellow cowling.

Unteroffizier Karl Nowak and Unteroffizier Johann Straub of 9./JG 2 on the yellow cowling of one of the Staffel's Bf 109 F-2s, Roquancourt, May–June 1941. Note the flares strapped to Nowak's leg and the map in Straub's boot.

Right: Better view of a typical Luftwaffe's fighter pilot's attire – Unteroffizier Karl Nowak, 9./JG 2, Roquancourt, May–June 1941.

Below: Oberleutnant Werner Stöckelmann, Gruppen Adjutant of III./JG 2. He would shoot down his first aircraft, a Spitfire, on 9 July 1941 and by the end of 1941 his score stood at three. However, he failed to score again and was killed in an accident on 29 May 1942. Twenty-six days later his replacement as Gruppen Adjutant, Oberleutnant Armin Faber, landed his brand-new Fw 190 A-3 in error at an RAF airfield in South Wales.

What appears to be a brand-new Bf 109 F of Stab III./JG 2. The vertical bar and Hahnkopf would indicate this as being the aircraft of Gruppen Kommandeur Hauptmann Hans Hahn. However, there are no victory bars on the tail, Hahn having forty-nine by the end of 1941. In September 1941, he was flying an F-4 Wk Nr 7185.

Werner Stöckelmann and a mechanic on the cowling of a 9./JG 2 Bf 109 F-4, Roquancourt, May–June 1941. Stöckelmann was originally in 9./JG 2 but III./JG 2 lost at least two Adjutants in the Battle of Britain so he could have been a replacement for Oberleutnant Erich Wolf who was killed on 29 October 1940.

Oberleutnant Werner Stöckelmann looks at the engine of a Bf 109 F-2; leaning on the wing to the left is Unteroffizier Karl Nowak, Roquancourt, May–June 1941.

Unteroffizier Karl Nowak with a Bf 109 F-2 of 9./JG 2. No Wk Nr or fuselage code is visible to identify this aircraft.

Werner Stöckelmann on what appears to be a pristine Bf 109 F-2, Roquancourt, May–June 1941.

Feldwebel Fritz Jahner's Bf 109 F-2 Yellow 8+I which was damaged in combat on 23 June 1941. No record of the Wk Nr was kept as the damage appears not to have been worth recording.

Unteroffizier Karl Nowak, Unteroffizier Johann Straub and Feldwebel Heinz Jahner, 9./JG 2, Roquancourt, May–June 1941.

Heinz Jahner on his Yellow 8+I, Roquancourt, May–June 1941.

Oberleutnant Erich Leie, Geschwader Adjutant of JG 2, in front of his Bf 109 F-4, St Pol-Brias, 17 October 1941. Four days previously, he had shot down his 29th aircraft. He would take command of I./JG 2 towards the end of June 1942 but would be wounded over Dieppe on 19 August 1942, not returning to operational duties until 2 October 1942. His score on 19 August 1942 rose to forty-three.

At 1230hrs on 6 November 1941, Oberfeldwebel Magnus 'Ghandi' Brunkhorst of 9./JG 2 shot down his third aircraft of the war, a Whirlwind. Only one Whirlwind was lost that day – serial P6970 of 263 Squadron flown by 21-year-old Sergeant John Robinson. Brunkhorst is seen here on his return, Feldwebel Karl Nowak is far right. He was flying a Bf 109 F-4 coded Yellow 5+I which is just visible.

Leutnant Leopold 'Poldi Wenger,' Oberfeldwebel Karl Pfeiffer and Leutnant Horst Walbeck of 3./JG 2. Wenger had only recently joined 3./JG 2. Pfeiffer, in front of whose aircraft they are standing, shot down aircraft numbers 9–11 on 18 December 1941 whilst Walbeck got his third that day. Wenger would be awarded the Ritterkreuz but was killed in action on 10 April 1945 with 6./SG 103, Pfeiffer would be killed in action with 5./JG 2 on 8 January 1943 whilst Walbeck would be killed in an accident on 7 May 1943 with 3./JG 77.

1942

This Bf 109 F-2 probably belongs to Erg.Jagdgruppe-Süd which was one of three fighter pools formed in 1942, as the pilot who took the photograph, Unteroffizier Werner Schammert, joined 10./JG 26 in the latter half of 1942 from this unit. Note the numerals painted just below the cockpit indicating that this is a training aircraft. The partial code of this aircraft is PD+O

A frontal view of the Erg.Jagdgruppe-Süd Bf 109 F-2 which would have been based in Mannheim-Sandhofen from its creation in February 1942 until October 1942 by which time Unteroffizier Schammert was with 10./JG 26.

Leutnant Leopold Wenger of 3./JG 2 in a Bf 109 F-4 coded Yellow 12 of 3./JG 2, Le Havre, 10 April 1942. Note the armoured windscreen and the aircraft maker's plate. Wenger flew two Alarmstarts or scrambles from Le Havre in this aircraft on 26 March 1942. His next was on 17 April 1942 by which time he was flying from Triqueville.

Wenger took this photo on the flight from Le Havre to Triqueville on 10 April 1942.

Believed to be from Oberleutnant Bruno Stolle's 8./JG 2, by May 1942 III./JG 2 had traded its Bf 109 F-2s for Fw 190 A-2s. In the background is Yellow 4 from Oberleutnant Siegfried Schnell's 9./JG 2. For most of the early part of 1942, III./JG 2 was based at Théville.

Bf 109 E-7 White 12 of Jagdgruppe Drontheim. Formed from JFS 3 mid-1941, the operational element was 4. (Eins.)/JGr Drontheim commanded by Oberleutnant Jürgen Waldheim and then from January 1942 by Oberleutnant Hans-Herbert Wulff. The shield of a black arrow on a white triangle inside a russet shield with a blue bar on top is usually associated with JFS 3 whilst the four-leaf clover, green inside a white diamond, is associated with IV./JG 5, Jagdgruppe Drontheim becoming 11./JG 5 at the end of June 1942.

Chocks away for Bf 109 E-7 White 12, Trondheim-Vaernes, spring 1942. The four-leaf clover is evident behind the spinner.

Believed to be Leutnant Oskar Ziesig in the cockpit of his Bf 109 F-4y of Hauptmann Günther Beise's I./JG 1, Jever, September 1942. The longer aerial indicates this aircraft was part of the Erprobungsschwarm responsible for trialling the use of the Y-Gerät navigation system which would then be installed in the Bf 109 G as a Morane antenna. Ziesig flew with 8./JG 2 in 1941, then I./JG 1 and finally 6./JG 51 and survived the war.

Bf 109 F-4s of the reconnaissance unit 1(F)./123. The first reported loss of an F-4 by this unit came on 28 August 1942 when Feldwebel Georg Fischer was shot down flying a Bf 109 F-4 Wk Nr 10188 coded White R by Wing Commander L. Mrazek (Exeter Wing Leader) and Squadron Leader L. E. Dolezal of 310 Squadron eight miles south of Exmouth. These two are coded White T and White O.

Leutnant Heinz Knoke joined 6./JG 52 in May 1941 but was posted to 3./JG 1 in July 1941. His first claim was not until 31 October 1942 but he would go on to claim thirty-three aircraft and was awarded the Deutsches Kreuz in Gold on 17 November 1942 and then the Ritterkreuz on 24 March 1945.

Bf 109 F-4s of 3./JG 2 at Leeuwarden, 19 February 1942. I./JG 2 had moved to the Pas de Calais in February 1943 in support of the Channel Dash by the warships *Prinz Eugen*, *Gneisenau* and *Scharnhorst* on 12 February 1942.

Bf 109 F-4 Yellow 12 of 3./JG 2, Katwijk, 14 February 1942. Two days previous, Leutnant Leopold Wenger (2nd from left) took off from Calais-Marck at 1545hrs to protect the German warships transitting the Dover Straits. He recorded a combat with Spitfires off Ostend but landed without incident at Katwijk at 1655hrs.

Bf 109 F-4 Yellow 6 of 3./JG 2, Le Havre, 9 April 1942. Note the black spinner and what appears to be a yellow nose on this aircraft.

Bf 109 F-4s of 3./JG 2 at Brest-Nord, winter 1941–2. Both aircraft have black spinners and yellow noses and the nearest aircraft is coded Yellow 4.

Leutnant Leopold Wenger on his Bf 109 F-4 Yellow 7, Triqueville, 15 April 1942. He would fly this aircraft on operations ten times, the last time being 19 May on 1942 before transferring to 10./JG 2 to become a Jabo pilot.

Stabsfeldwebel Erwin 'Icke' Kley of 11./JG 2 was an experienced fighter pilot. He had shot down four aircraft by the end of 1940 but would only shoot down another four in 1941. In May 1942, 11./JG 2 was formed as a high-altitude Staffel with the Bf 109 G-1 led by Oberleutnant Rudi Pflanz, and Kley transferred to it. He claimed his 14th victory over the Somme Estuary at 1500hrs on 31 July 1942; Pflanz claimed his 52nd aircraft shortly afterwards but was then shot down and killed, possibly by Sergeant Bill Kelly of 121 Squadron who claimed a Bf 109 near Le Crotoy. At 1600hrs on 19 August 1942, Kley was shot down flying a Bf 109 G-1, Wk Nr 10311 White 10, and was killed crash-landing at Le Tréport.

By the end of 1942, the Bf 109 F had been replaced by the Fw 190 or newer marks of Bf 109. This Bf 109 F of 3./JFS 4 (later JG 104) was photographed at Fürth in 1943.

Unteroffizier Robert Spreckels of 8./JG 1 claimed his first aircraft, a Boston of 107 Squadron, 30km west of Helgoland at 1756hrs on 1 August 1942. His next claim did not come until 22 March 1943 and he would only shoot down another two aircraft after that in 1942. Spreckels' claim to fame is that at just after midday on 25 June 1944 and flying a Fw 190 of the Alarmstaffel./JG 11 he shot down his second of two Mosquitoes over Jutland (his eighth kill), a 21 Squadron aircraft flying with 305 Squadron and crewed by Wing Commander Bob Braham DSO** DFC** and Flight Lieutenant Don Walsh, both of whom were captured.

Leutnant Heinz Knoke's Bf 109 F-4y Black 1, Jever, September 1942. The elongated aerial indicates this aircraft as flying with the Erprobungsschwarm equipped with Y-Gerät.

A Bf 109 F-4y of the Erprobungsschwarm/JG 1 – note the armoured windscreen and elongated aerial.

The nearest aircraft is believed to be the Bf 109 F-4 flown by Hauptmann Wolfram Phillips of Stab./JG 2, Abbeville-Drucat, spring 1942. Phillips would be shot down 10km north-west of Abbeville on 5 June 1942, flying Wk Nr 7658, and baled out wounded. Another loss was Unteroffizier Fritz Herke of 1./JG 2 flying a Bf 109 F-4 Wk Nr 8338. The only claims for these two aircraft are by Sergeant E. S. Hughes and Flight Lieutenant E. N. Woods of 72 Squadron and Squadron Leader E. H Thomas of 133 Squadron who claimed a Bf 109 probable. Hughes was the only pilot reporting seeing a parachute.

An unidentified Oberfeldwebel of the Erprobungsschwarm I./JG 1 in his Bf 109 F-4y. Note the JG 1 badge – silver arrow, black cross, white shield, red surround

1943

Leutnant Paul Müngersdorf climbing out of his Bf 109 G-1 at JFS 4, Fürth. After 19 March 1943, this unit became 3./JG 104. Note the three-digit fuselage code. He would be posted to II./JG 2 later in 1943.

Bf 109 G-6/R6 of 3./JG 27 at Fels am Wagram, August 1943. The Gruppe at this time was commanded by Hauptmann Ludwig Franzisket and was based at this airfield from the end of August 1943 until the Allied invasion of Normandy in June 1944.

For the first seven months of 1943, I./JG 27 was based in France. This photograph of what appears to be a Bf 109 G-4 of 1./JG 27 coded White 22 was reported to have been taken at Bernay, their base from 31 January to 14 April 1943, 1 Staffel being commanded by Oberleutnant Hans Remmer.

This Bf 109 G-6, Wk Nr 160811 PP+WO, was used for FuG 217 Neptun trials at Werneuchen, autumn 1943. Neptun was the code name of a series of low-to-mid-VHF band airborne-intercept radar systems.

Bf 109 G-6, Wk Nr 160811 PP+WO, at Werneuchen. Clearly visible are the FuG 217 Neptun aerials on the fuselage.

This Bf 109 G-6 White 28 of 4./JG 2 was reportedly flown by Leutnant Paul Müngersdorf in 1943. However, he flew initially with Stab II./JG 2 and then 5./JG 2, the latter having black not white codes. This aircraft, Wk Nr 19877, was lost with 5./JG 2 on 19 August 1943.

Oberleutnant Heinz Knoke's Bf 109 G-1, Black 1 of 5./JG 11 photographed at Jever in August 1943. By now, Knoke commanded 5./JG 11 and his score stood at twelve. He would shoot down a B-17 on 17 August 1943 to raise his score to thirteen but in this combat, his Bf 109 G-6, Wk Nr 15623 Black 1, was damaged and he force-landed at Rheinbach.

Opposite: Leutnant Hans-Joachim 'Hajo' Rimarski of 5./JG 2 shot down his first and only victory, a Spitfire at 0900hrs near Bourney, on 14 July 1943. His was one of four claimed by II./JG 2, the RAF losing three Spitfires with another one returning badly damaged. Just after midday on 19 August 1943, II./JG 2 was scrambled to intercept the second part of Ramrod 209 of B-26s attacking Poix. Although II./JG 2 accounted for three Spitfires, Rimarski flying a Bf 109 G-6, Wk Nr 19877 White 28, was shot down as was Unteroffizier Heinrich Köckler of 4./JG 2 in Bf 109 G-6, Wk Nr 15288, which crashed at Auxi-le-Château, killing Köckler and Unteroffizier Gustav Sens of 5./JG 2 who baled out wounded from his Bf 109 G-6, Wk Nr 15387, near Epinoy. The only claims for Bf 109s at that time and location were by 341 Squadron (Bf 109 damaged near Amiens) and 403 and 485 Squadron (Bf 109 destroyed by each). Rimarski was killed when his Bf 109 crashed near Talmas, north-east of Amiens, so was possibly a victim of either Flight Lieutenant Martin Hume of 485 Squadron (whose victim exploded) or Flight Lieutenant Arthur Coles of 403 Squadron.

Leutnant Paul Müngersdorf's Bf 109 G-6, Wk Nr 15781 Black 7+-, photographed at Poix, July–August 1943.

On 12 August 1943, the same Black 7 suffered engine trouble and force-landed near Aachen.

Leutnant Paul Müngersdorf looks down at his Black 7 which was reported as suffering 60 per cent damage in the crash-landing near Aachen on 12 August 1943.

The last moments of a Bf 109 G about to be shot down by Lieutenant Leroy W. Ista flying a P-47 D of the 352nd Fighter Squadron, 353rd Fighter Group USAAF near Gelsenkirchen, 1320hrs, 5 November 1943. It is possible that his victim was Unteroffizier Robert Pautner of 9./JG 26 who baled out wounded from his Bf 109 G-6, Wk Nr 15408 White 12, near Gelsenkirchen-Buer. Ista was reported missing on 22 December 1943 when his P-47 D serial 42-22458 was crashed in the English Channel 10 miles off the coast.

In the summer of 1943, Bf 109s and Fw 190s were used for night-fighter sorties, known as Wilde Sau (Wild Boar) missions. Although staged for propaganda, this Bf 109 F gives an idea of the preparations for such sorties.

The Bf 109 G-6 flown by Feldwebel Arnold Döring of 2./JG 300, summer 1943. His first Wilde Sau victory was reported as being the night of 27 September 1943. Döring was originally a bomber pilot, joining 9./KG 55 at the end of the Battle of Britain. With 9./KG 55 on the Eastern Front, he and his crew were then credited with shooting down seven Soviet fighters by day and three bombers by night. Converting to the Bf 109 and Wilde Sau and later more traditional night fighters, it is believed he shot down another ten aircraft at night and two by day. He would be awarded the Ritterkreuz and survived the war.

JG 50 was formed at Wiesbaden-Erbenheim from Jagdgruppe Süd Oberbefehlshaber der Luftwaffe (OBdL) in mid-August 1943 under the leadership of Major Hermann Graf. Graf's first victory did not come until 4 August 1941 when he was flying with 9./JG 52. By the end of 1941, his score stood at forty-eight and he would be awarded the Ritterkreuz on 24 January 1942. He would then receive the Eichenlaub on 17 May 1942 by which time his score stood at 105; he would receive the Schwerter two days later. On 16 September 1942, he would shoot down his 173rd and 174th aircraft and would receive the Brillanten. At the end of January 1943, he took command of the training unit Jagdgruppe Ost but six months later took command of Jagdgruppe Süd OBdL, a high-altitude anti-Mosquito unit. He would get three more victories with JG 50 but on 16 December 1943, took command of JG 1 where he took his score to 212, his final victory being a P-51 on 29 March 1944 after which he collided with another P-51 and was forced to baled out wounded from his Bf 109 G-6, Wk Nr 26020 Black<<+. This photograph shows Graf with his Bf 109 G-6, Wk Nr 15913 Green 1, of JG 50 at Weisbaden-Erbenheim, September 1943.

1944–1945

Unteroffizier Hans Seyringer of 4./JG 27 joined his unit in July 1943. He would claim a USAAF B-17 north of Kaiserslautern at 1413hrs on 14 October 1943 and his second, and last, kill was a P-47 near Borkelt on 30 January 1944. Immediately afterwards, another P-47 (presumed to be his victim's wingman) shot him down, his Bf 109 G-6, Wk Nr 410300 White 5 (seen here), crashing 8–10km west of Twente, Seyringer baling out wounded; he then recalls meeting who he thought he shot down in hospital a few days later. A P-47 D 42-75567 of 374th Fighter Squadron/361 Fighter Group did crash at Borkelt but 1st Lieutenant Ethelbert Amason was killed. However, P-47D 42-74621 flown by 2nd Lieutenant Edwin Mead of 335th Fighter Squadron/4 Fighter Group is reported to have crashed near Haaksbergen and he was captured. The 335th Fighter Squadron claimed a number of Bf 109s destroyed, probably destroyed or damaged in the Lingen area whilst the 374th Fighter Squadron claimed similar in the Rheine area.

Seen at Weisbaden-Erbenheim, late 1943 are three pilots of 4./JG 27. Left to right: Unteroffizier Hans Seyringer, Oberfeldwebel Alfred Müller and Unteroffizier Konstanin Benzien, all three of whom would become casualties. Benzien was reported missing in action on 11 December 1943 near Groningen/ Opeinde flying Bf 109 G-6, Wk Nr 410298 White 6. Seyringer would be wounded in action when he was shot down near Twente on 30 January 1944 flying a Bf 109 G-6, Wk Nr 410300 White 5, whilst Müller would be shot down and wounded in action on 8 April 1944, baling out of Bf 109 G-6, Wk Nr 440730 White 4, near Wesendorf. Benzien had no victories and Seyringer two victories. Müller was more successful getting his seventh and eighth on the day he was shot down. He would then increase his score to sixteen between 14 July and 7 August 1944 before he was shot down and killed near Issinghausen on 16 August 1944 flying Bf 109 G-6/AS, Wk Nr 412556 White 9. In the back ground nearest the camera is the Bf 109 G-6 of Gruppen Kommandeur Hauptmann Werner Schroer and a Bf 109 G-6 White 8 of 4./JG 27. It is possible White 8 was Wk Nr 162893 which was shot down near Zethlingen on 28 May 1944, the pilot Unteroffizier Gerhard Franke being killed.

A Bf 109 G-6 of III./JG 26 either seen at Villacoublay in June 1944 or Lille in September 1944. Markings are white which would indicate 7./JG 26 but in October 1943, 6./JG 26 became 7./JG 26 and part of II./JG 26 whilst 7./JG 26 became 9./JG 26 in III./JG 26 which it is believed this aircraft comes from. 9./JG 26 was commanded by Oberleutnant Viktor Hilgendorff (killed in action south of Dreux in Bf 109 G-6, 413482, White 3) and then Oberleutnant Gottfried Schmidt.

Photographed at Creil is this Bf 109 G-6 of 5./JG 2. The pilot is Oberleutnant Gerd Schaedle, Staffelführer of 5 Staffel. He had previously flown with JG 3 and took over the Staffel after Oberleutnant Georg Eder was injured in an accident on 5 November 1943. Schaedle would be shot down in combat on 29 January 1944, his Bf 109 G-6, Wk Nr 20741, crashing at Longivilly near Bastogne and he baled out wounded. He would be shot down again at 1445hrs on 6 March 1944 near Hopsten by three P-47s of 368th Fighter Squadron/355th Fighter Group apparently flown by Captain Walter Koraleski, 1st Lieutenant Norman Fortier and Flight Officer Clarence Barger. This time he would be uninjured. He would survive the war and was credited with nine victories.

Seen at Wien-Seyring in April–May 1944 are these Bf 109 G-6/R6s of 9./JG 27. The second aircraft from the right is Wk Nr 441090 flown by Staffelkapitän Leutnant Dr Peter Werfft who would be shot down and wounded flying this aircraft whilst engaged in a transfer flight to Gardelegen on 19 May 1944. Werfft had joined 3./JG 27 in June 1940 as a Gefreiter, his first two victories coming on 27 September 1940. On 19 May 1944, he had had just shot down two B-24s for his 21st and 22nd victories before he was shot down and wounded. His wounds meant he did not rejoin JG 27 until October 1944, then taking command of III Gruppe. He would be awarded the Ritterkreuz in January 1945 and survived the war.

Hard to spot but this is a Bf 10-9 G-6 of Oberleutnant Lothar Gerlach's 1./JG 5 camouflaged at Moislains-Chauny airstrip, June–July 1944. This aircraft was flown by Unteroffizier Johannes Geilert and is presumed to be Wk Nr 412612 White 4. Geilert was flying this aircraft on the afternoon of 15 July 1944 and was shot down by Flak, baling out to be captured and his aircraft crashed at Villons-Les Buissons, north-west of Caen.

An unusual variant was the Bf 109 G-12 two-seat aircraft. This is the 52nd prototype, Bf 109 CJ+MG formerly Bf 109 G-6/Trop Wk Nr 19319.

This photograph gives few clues apart from that the aircraft are Bf 109 G-6s, probably from JG 3. The lack of any markings after the fuselage cross would possibly indicate I Gruppe and as the markings ahead of the second aircraft's fuselage cross is white, it could be 1./JG 3. In 1944, 1 Staffel would suffer four Staffelkapitän killed, one wounded and one posted to command I./JG 3. Those who were casualties were mainly flying the G-6 but one was flying a G-5 and one a G-14.

Seen hiding from Allied aircraft at Evreux on 7 June 1944 is this Bf 109 G-6 <1+- of Stab II./JG 3. The pilot of this aircraft is believed to be Oberleutnant Max-Bruno Fischer, the Gruppen Adjutant. He apparently survived the war and was credited with three victories. Note the 'Udet' badge on the cowling.

2./NAGr 13 would convert from the Fw 190 to the Bf 109 G-6 and then the G-8 in mid-1944 and would move from Cuers in southern France back to Landsberg in Germany at the end of August 1944. This photograph was taken before the move as the officer seated left, Leutnant Georg Pemmler, was badly wounded in an attack by the Resistance north of Villars on the road from Lyon to Bourg whilst travelling by road back to Germany. Between 21 and 28 August 1944, a total of two from this unit were killed, six captured and ten wounded. In the centre seated is believed to be Staffelkapitän Hauptmann Roland Eckerscham who would hand over to Hauptmann Wilhelm Messner in June 1944.

With its national markings painted over, this is Bf 109 G-14, Wk Nr 462919 White 7+I. It is believed that this photograph was taken at Eperstedt in November 1944 and that the pilot of this aircraft was Ritterkreuz winner Oberleutnant Oskar 'Ossi' Romm. In 1944, Romm flew with 2./JG 51, IV./JG 3, 12./JG 3, 15./JG 3 and in November 1944 4./JG 3. He would command IV./JG 3 from February 1945 until he was injured in an accident on 24 April 1945. His final score would be ninety-two aircraft shot down in combat.

Reported as shot down in southern Jutland, Denmark in spring 1945, all that can be said for certain is that this is a Regensburg-built Bf 109 G-6 which appears to have the marking Yellow 6. It is possible that the unit is 3./EJG 1 which was based at Hadersleben, Denmark from January 1945 until the end of the war.

This Bf 109 G-6 or G-8 of 2./Erg.Aufklärungsgeschwader 1 coded Red 20 is an unusual aircraft. It also carries the code N5+UK which is 2./NAGr Bromberg, I./ Erg.Aufklärungsgeschwader 1 being formed from this unit and based at Bromberg in January 1945 under the command of Major Ludwig Holler, a very experienced reconnaissance pilot who had been flying operationally since the start of the war.

Feldwebel Günther Parge sitting on the nose of a Bf 109 G-12 of 4./KG(J) 6, Prague-Klecany, December 1944. In October 1944, II./KG 6, commanded by Hauptmann Joachim Faulhaber, handed over its Ju 88s and began converting to a fighter unit. 308 is the last three digits of the werk nummer, believed to be 161308.

Feldwebel Günther Parge of 4./KG(J) 6 sitting in the cockpit of a Bf 109 K-4/R6 White 1, Klecany, January–March 1945. On his left arm is a yellow armband with a Luftwaffe eagle and the words 'Deutsche Luftwaffe', used to show that should he have to bale out, he was German and not a 'Terrorflieger'

These Bf 109 G-6s were captured at Fassberg at the end of the war. All seem to have been refurbished and have new and unusual camouflage but no codes.

Seen at Fassberg is this Bf 109 G-6, Wk Nr 20790, the Wk Nr visible on the tail in other photographs.

A close-up of Wk Nr 20790's nose shows the hastily-applied camouflage.

A line-up of at least three Bf 109s and two Fw 190s, Flensburg, 1945. The nearest Bf 109 is a G-14/AS coded Yellow 62.

The scene at Danzig, 1 March 1945. The holed Bf 109 G-14 nearest the camera is Wk Nr 510959 which is just visible on the tail. The unit is believed to have been Stab./JG 51 and the code would either be Green or Yellow 4.

Nine Bf 109s are seen at Johannistal/Adlershof, May 1945. Most appear to be Erla-built Bf 109 G-6s. The nearest aircraft has Wk Nr 4126095 stencilled on the lower rudder and the numeral 13 on the fuselage. The aircraft behind it is Wk Nr 414757.

This Bf 109 K-4 Wk Nr 612802 is seen at the railway station at Tišnov north of Brno in what is now the Czech Republic. There was a production line at Tišnov hidden in a railway tunnel. (via Z. Hurt)

This Bf 109 K-4 coded 7+I was found at Prague-Kbely airfield at the end of the war. It is believed this was Wk Nr 331??? from 10./JG 27. (via Z. Hurt)

JABO

Armourers loading 50kg bombs onto a Bf 109. At least two bombs are visible, the ETC 500 bomb rack being capable of carrying four under the fuselage.

This Bf 109 F-4/B coded Blue 2+<- of 10./JG 2 is seen at Caen-Carpiquet on 4 June 1942. Sister unit 10./JG 26 used a stylized diagonal white bomb after the fuselage cross on its Bf 109 Fs.

Oberfeldwebel Gerhard Limberg (left) and Leutnant Leopold Wenger (right) were two successful Jabo pilots with 10./JG 2. Limberg was awarded the Ehrenpokal as a Leutnant on 26 July 1943 and the Deutsches Kreuz in Gold on 20 March 1944. He would survive the war, joining the Bundesluftwaffe afterwards and retiring as the Inspector General of the Luftwaffe in 1978. Wenger would be awarded the Deutsches Kreuz in Gold on 17 October 1943 and the Ritterkreuz on 14 January 1945 but was killed in action on 10 April 1945.

Practice 50kg bombs (indicated by the white noses) on a Bf 109 F of 10./JG 26, St Omer-Arques. This unit was based at Arques from its creation on 10 March 1942 until 26 May that year.

The 10./JG 2 badge was a russet-coloured fox carrying a grey-blue ship and used on its Bf 109s and Fw 190s. It was later used by II./SG 10 on the Eastern Front where a Soviet star was added to the right of the ship.

The 10./JG 26 bomb painted aft of the fuselage cross on this Bf 109 F-4/B at Arques, spring 1942. When the Staffel converted to the Fw 190, the bomb was painted horizontally, smaller and black and white.

Awkward working conditions loading dummy bombs onto this Bf 109 F-4/B of 10./JG 26 at Arques, spring 1942.

Opposite: Armourers attaching the 50kg bomb shackle to load it onto the ETC 500 bomb rack of this Bf 109.

Hauptmann Frank Liesendahl, Staffelkapitän of 10./ JG 2, getting out of the cockpit of his Bf 109 F-4/B. A great exponent of the Jabo, he was awarded the Deutsches Kreuz in Gold (which he is wearing) on 5 June 1942. Shortly after this photograph was taken, 10./JG 2 converted to the Fw 190 and Liesendahl was shot down and killed on 17 July 1942. He would be awarded the Ritterkreuz posthumously.

Liesendahl in his Bf 109 F-4/B, Wk Nr 7629, Blue 1+<-, Beaumont-le Roger, 31 March 1942. The spinner is black, rudder yellow and underneath the engine yellow.

The rudder of Liesendahl's Wk Nr 7629 showing anti-shipping successes on 17 May and 9 June 1941 (both with 6./JG 2) and 23 March, 27 March, 2 May and 7 June 1942.

Liesendahl admiring his handiwork shortly before trading in his Bf 109 F-4/B for a Fw 190 A-2, mid-June 1942.

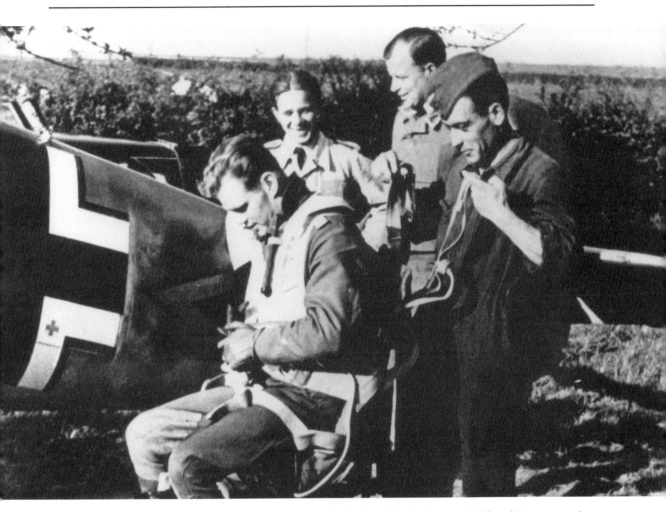

Liesendahl preparing for another mission; by the tail is believed to be Leutnant Erhard Nippa, another successful Jabo pilot who would be awarded the Deutsches Kreuz in Gold on 29 April 1943 and the Ritterkreuz on 26 March 1944; he would survive the war.

An F-4/B of 10./JG 2 clearly showing the positioning of the fox badge. Spinner is black and it can be seen that the underneath of the engine is yellow.

A Bf 109 F-4/B, Wk Nr 8352 White 2, of 10./JG 26. This photograph was probably taken at Caen-Carpiquet as 10 Staffel was based there from 26 March to 18 June 1942 before moving to Le Bourget to convert to the Fw 190. (Via ECPA/Caldwell).

Wk Nrs 8344, 8345, 8351 and 8361 are recorded as being with 10./JG 26. On 6 June 1942, Feldwebel Otto Görtz was shot down by Flak off Bournemouth flying a Bf 109 F-4/B White 2 but Wk Nr 8532. It is believed that this Wk Nr is an error and should in fact be 8352. (Via ECPA/Caldwell)

Bf 109 F-4/B White 9 of 10./JG 26. The only aircraft lost by this Staffel were White 2 (Wk Nr 8352), White 7 (Wk Nr 8344) and White 11 (Wk Nr 7232).

Wk Nr 7232 White 11 was hit by Flak attacking shipping off Newhaven and force-landed at Beachy Head at 1205hrs on 20 May 1942. Unteroffizier Oswald Fischer was captured.

RAF mechanics inspect the engine. The aircraft was recovered, fitted with a new engine and propeller and flew as NN644 under British ownership.

The Jabo that was not. Bf 109 G-1 WkNr 14008, BD+GC was a long-range fighter bomber (Jagdbomber mit vergrösserter Reichweite or Jaborei) prototype with jettisonable additional landing gear so that it could be fitted with drop tanks and in this case a 500kg bomb.

THE MEDITERRANEAN
AND NORTH AFRICA

The introduction of the Bf 109 E-7 did not come until the latter stages of the Battle of Britain, too late to make an impact. Essentially the same as the Bf 109 E-4, it could also be powered by the DB 601N engine and was fitted with a 300-litre drop tank which almost doubled its range and thus made it ideal for operations over the Mediterranean in 1941. These are Fieseler-built Bf 109 E-7s, the closest two aircraft being coded VL+AH and VL+AL.

In January 1941, it was decided that 7./JG 26, commanded by Oberleutnant Joachim Müncheberg, would be moved to the Mediterranean to operate with the Bf 110s of Major Karl Kaschka's III./ZG 26. A black and white spinner, yellow cowling, red heart and Schlageter badge under the canopy identifies this as an E-7 of 7./JG 26. In the background is a Bf 110 C coded 3U+FT of Hauptmann Roland Borth's 9./ZG 76. Note the white fuselage bands.

Another unit on its way to the Balkans and the Mediterranean was Hauptmann Max Dobislav's III./JG 27. This unit was unique in that tactical markings were on the nose. This aircraft is of the Gruppe Adjutant, possibly Leutnant Rolf Seitz, and is seen at Kozani between 16 and 26 April 1941.

Bf 109 E-7, Wk Nr 4187 Yellow 5, flown by the Staffelkapitän of 9./JG 27 Oberleutnant Erbo Graf von Kageneck, Gela, Sicily, May 1941. By October 1940, this pilot had shot down thirteen aircraft. He would add another four over Malta between 6 and 20 May 1941. In June 1941, III./JG 27 moved to the Russian Front and by 12 October 1941, von Kaganeck's score had risen to sixty-five. He would be awarded the Ritterkreuz on 30 July 1941 and the Eichenlaub on 26 October 1941 by which time III./JG 27 had moved to North Africa. However, he would only get another two victories on 12 December 1941 before he was mortally wounded in combat with RAF fighters near Agedabia on 24 December 1941 flying Bf 09 F-4 Trop Wk Nr 8554 and would die on 12 January 1942.

Major Gotthard Handrick's III./JG 52 (until January 1941 it was I./JG 28) was based in Bucharest-Pipera from 14 October 1940 to 20 May 1941 and then again on 12 June 1941. In the interim period, it operated over Greece. It claimed no victories during this time and suffered just accidents. This line-up of E-7s is from Oberleutnant Franz Hörnig's 9./JG 52. Shortly afterwards, III./JG 52 converted to the Bf 109 F-4 which it would operate over the Soviet Union from 22 June 1941 onwards.

On 14 May 1941, this Bf 109 E-7, Wk Nr 6435 <<+~, of Stab III./JG 77 suffered Flak damage over Maleme and crash-landed at Molaoi on its return. Strangely, the cowling does not have the usual wolf's-head badge of III./JG 77 but what appears to be the red cartoon sparrow of 8./JG 54.

Leutnant Diethelm von Eichel-Streiber, Gruppen Adjutant of III./JG 77, stands by the tail of his Wk Nr 6435, 14 May 1941.

Von Eichel-Streiber was originally a bomber pilot and was awarded the Spanish Cross in Gold with Swords for his time with the Condor Legion. He joined III./JG 52 in 1941 and in 1941 was the Adjutant to his uncle Major Alexander von Winterfeldt, Gruppen Kommandeur of III./ JG 77. He scored his first kill on the day this photograph was taken, a Hurricane over Maleme at 0631hrs, his uncle getting a Gladiator for his sixth victory two minutes later. He would go on to shoot down ninety-six aircraft, was awarded the Ritterkreuz and Deutsches Kreuz in Gold and survived the war.

Bf 109 E-7s of 9./JG 27. The nearest aircraft is coded 1, the next 8 and are believed to be at Gela between 5 and 20 May 1941.

The chevron on the cowling of this Bf 109 E-7 identifies this as the aircraft of Hauptmann Max Dobislav, Gruppen Kommandeur of III./JG 27. This photograph is believed to have been taken in April 1941 by which time he had eight victories. His ninth would be over Malta on 15 May 1941. The Wk Nr is believed to be 5596. He would survive the war having achieved fifteen victories but the only major award he received was the Ehrenpokal on 3 November 1941.

Photographed at Catania on 17 April 1941 on their way to North Africa are pilot of 1./JG 27. Left to right: Feldwebel Werner Lange (+23 April 1941), Oberleutnant Wolfgang Redlich (Staffelkapitän +29 May 1944; awarded Ritterkreuz), Oberleutnant Hugo Schneider (+11 January 1942), unidentified Bf 110 pilot, Leutnant Eugen von Moller, Feldwebel Emil Kaiser (wounded 21 November 1941), Feldwebel Albert Espenlaub (POW 13 December 1941 but shot trying to escape 25 February 1942), Oberfeldwebel Gerhard Otto (wounded 9 May 1941).

Leutnant Werner Schroer became Gruppen Adjutant of I./JG 27 from 1./JG 27 by which time his score stood at seven victories. His eighth came on 30 May 1942 but on 30 June 1942 he took command of 8./JG 27. He would survive the war with 114 victories, having been awarded the Ritterkreuz, Eichenlaub, Deutsches Kreuz in Gold and Ehrenpokal.

A Rotte of Bf 109 E-7s. The badge on the nose identifies the lead aircrsft as White 5 of 1./JG 27. Leutnant Werner Schroer was injured in combat on 21 April 1941 and landed Bf 109 E-7, Wk Nr 4170 White 3, at Ain-el-Gazala but it is believed this photograph was taken later than this. I./JG 27 would convert to the Bf 109 F-4 in October 1941.

Loading a Bf 109 E-7 Yellow 2 of 9./JG 27 with a 250kg bomb for a Jabo attack on Malta, May 1941.

With the cowling off of this III./JG 27 Bf 109 E-7, the only clue to its identity is the nine victory marks on the tail which would indicate it to be the aircraft of Kommandeur Hauptmann Max Dobislav who would get his ninth on 15 May 1941 and then the tenth on 6 July 1941. The photograph was taken at Gela which was the III Gruppe base until 20 May 1941.

A Bf 109 E-7 caught strafing Menidi, Athens, on 21 April 1941. The unit responsible is believed to be II or III./JG 77 which between 0845 and 1000hrs on that day sent thirty-one Bf 109s, four of them acting as Jabos, to attack the airfields at Tatoi and Eleusis. RAF records confirm that Menidi, the base for Blenheims of 11, 84, 113 and 211 Squadrons, was strafed by twelve Bf 109s that morning, several Blenheims being damaged, one beyond repair. The following day, the RAF moved out. One 211 Squadron NCO, Sergeant 'Jimmy' Riddle, wrote 'The 109s knocked the hell out of us at Menidi . . .' (via D. R. Neate)

Bf 109 E-7, Wk Nr 1809, White 2 of Oberleutnant Erhard Braune's 7./JG 27, Romania, February 1941. Note what appears to be one victory bar at the base of the tail.

Bf 109 E-4/B Black 5 of Oberleutnant Hans Lass' 8./JG 27, Gela, May 1941. Lass took command of 8 Staffel when Oberleutnant Arno Becker was shot down in combat on 6 April 1941. A Bf 109 E-4/B, Wk Nr 2025 Black 2, was lost near Soty in the Soviet Union on 28 June 1941, Unteroffizier Gerhard Sdun returned safely only to be killed flying a Bf 109 G-6, Wk Nr 16650 of 12./JG 27 near Maleme on 26 May 1943.

Oberleutnant Ludwig Franzisket was the Gruppen Adjutant of I./JG 27 from the start of October 1940 to 5 December 1941 when he took over 1./JG 27 from Hauptmann Wolfgang Redlich. However, records state he was flying with 3./JG 27 from 26 June 1941 as on that date he got his 20th victory, the award of the Ritterkreuz coming on 23 July 1941 by which time he had twenty-two victories. He was back with Stab I./JG 27 in September 1941 and his first victory with 1./JG 27 was his 25th and 26th on 17 December 1941. He would survive the war with forty-three victories. This photograph was taken in April 1941, probably at Ain-el-Gazala, I Gruppe's base from 21 April 1941 until December 1941.

Unteroffizier Gerhard Beitz joined 9./JG 53 in November 1941 and shot down his first aircraft, a Hurricane possibly from 126 Squadron, over Malta on 9 March 1942 on his 21st operational flight. This shows Beitz taxying back in Comiso at 1550hrs in Bf 109 F-4 Yellow 11+I.

Ground crew rush to congratulate Beitz, Comiso, 9 March 1942.

Beitz looks pleased with himself. He would shoot down a Spitfire (possibly flown by Pilot Officer Norman Fowlow who baled out wounded into the sea and was rescued together with Unteroffizier Johannes Lompa of 4./JG 53 whose Bf 109 F-4, Wk Nr 7596 White 1, had been shot down off Hal Far) on the late morning of 18 May 1942 only to be shot down himself, possibly by Pilot Officer John Bisley of 126 Squadron or Pilot Officer T. W. Scott of 126 Squadron, 10km south of Marsa Scirocco in Bf 109 F-4, Wk Nr 8670 Yellow 2+I. Landing in the sea near the Island of Filfi, he was not rescued until 21 May 1942.

This Bf 109 G-2, Wk Nr 13633 White 1, flown by Hauptmann Wolf-Dietrich Huy Staffelkapitän of 7./ JG 77 was photographed at Bari on either 23 or 24 October 1942, showing thirty-nine of his forty kills. Huy's first kill came on 31 May 1940 with Stab II./Jagdgruppe186 (Träger) and he would get his 40th on 28 October 1942 but was then shot down the following day by Flying Officer John Nicholls of 601 Squadron near El Alamein whilst flying this aircraft and taken prisoner. Huy had been awarded the Ritterkreuz on 5 July 1941 and the Eichenlaub on 17 March 1942.

Unteroffizier Felix Sauer had joined 3./JG 53 in October 1940 only to move to 6./JG 53. In 1942, he was a member of Oberleutnant Werner Langemann's 10 (Jabo)./JG 53 which was formed in February 1942 and would later become 1./Jabogruppe Afrika. On 16 May 1942 his Bf 109 F-4, Wk Nr 7282 White 6, suffered engine failure and he baled out over the sea 65km south of Pozzalo. He was picked up eight days and seven nights later by the Italian torpedo boat *Turbine*. He would survive the war.

A Bf 109 F-4 from 9./JG 53, Comiso, 1942. From September 1940 to October 1942 the Staffel was commanded by Oberleutnant Franz Götz

Oberstleutnant Eduard Neumann commanded JG 27 from 10 June 1942 to 22 April 1943. Prior to that, he had commanded I./JG 27 from July 1940. His final score was said to be eleven aircraft which was not enough to get him the Ritterkreuz although he was awarded the Deutsches Kreuz in Gold on 11 May 1942. This photograph of him in his Bf 109 F-4 was either taken at Tmimi or Sidi Barani in June 1942.

This Bf 109 G-6 Trop has clues as to its identity. Just visible is the Pik As badge of JG 53 and on the propeller blade its Wk Nr 16327. This aircraft was badly damaged in an accident at Sciacca on 22 May 1943 and its remains discovered by the Allies after the airfield was occupied after 13 July 1943.

A Bf 109 G-7 Trop White 2+I of 7./JG 27 flown by Staffelkapitän Leutnant Emil Clade, one of four aircraft escorting a He 111 carrying Generals Alexander Holle and Martin Fiebig to Crete, 1 December 1943. Clade had joined III./JG 27 during the Battle of Britain and would go on to claim twenty-six victories. He would be awarded the Ehrenpokal on 20 March 1944 and would survive the war. (via Clade)

A Bf 109 G-6 Trop Black 16 of 8./JG 53, Sicily, spring–summer 1943. For much of this period, 8 Staffel was commanded by Hauptmann Franz Schiess. Schiess had joined Stab./JG 53 in March 1941 as the Geschwader Adjutant and moved to command 8./JG 53 in February 1943, his score standing at thirty-seven for which he was awarded the Ritterkreuz on 21 June 1943. He was reported missing in combat with B-25s and P-38s near Ischia on 2 June 1943 whilst flying Bf 109 G-6, Wk Nr 160022 Black 1+I, his victory total being sixty-seven.

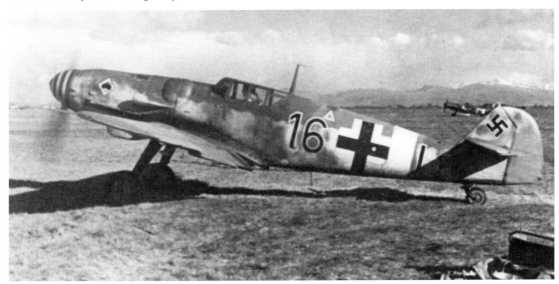

An unidentified Bf 109 G-6 of 8./JG 53. Note that on this and the previous photograph the aircraft have spiral-painted spinners.

These Bf 109 G-4s of 4./JG 53 are posed for the cameras at La Marsa. The middle aircraft is White 4 of Staffelkapitän Oberleutnant Fritz Dinger and the next aircraft along is believed to be White 5 of Oberfeldwebel Stefan Litjens whose rudder shows two rows of ten and one of nine victories, his 29th being a Spitfire on 6 December 1942. Dinger (the tall officer 4th from right) had been awarded the Ritterkreuz on 23 December 1942 and would be killed in a bombing attack on Scalea on 27 July 1943, his score standing at sixty-seven. Litjens, who would fly with 4./JG 53 throughout the war, always favoured White 5+I and would be awarded the Ritterkreuz on 21 June 1943. He would survive the war, his score standing at thirty-eight.

Throughout the North African campaign, many German aircraft were discovered or captured. This is a Bf 109 F-4 Trop White 9+I of Hauptmann Wilfried Pufahl's 7./JG 53 found at Quotaifiya.

Another view of White 9 showing the stylized numeral and a lack of Perspex front canopy and of the middle and rear canopy sections.

This Bf 109 F-4 Trop, Wk Nr 8477 White 5, of 1./JG 27 is seen at El Adem on 22 December 1941. Damaged in combat on 13 December 1941, it force-landed at El Adem. (Group Captain Pell-Fry via Thomas)

The pilot of White 5 was Oberfeldwebel Albert Espenlaub. His first victory was a Hurricane over Tobruk on 21 April 1941 and by the time of his capture on 13 December 1941, his score stood at fourteen, his last victory being a Blenheim on 11 December 1941. He would be shot and killed trying to escape from captivity on 25 February 1942.

Starboard view of Oberfeldwebel Albert Espenlaub's White 5 showing clearly showing the I./JG 27 lioness-over-Africa emblem on the cowling.

This F-4 Trop Yellow 2 is from Leutnant Klaus Faber's 9./JG 27 and was brought back to flying condition at Derna in January 1942 by 1 Squadron South African Air Force (SAAF).

This F-4 Trop White 6+I is from 7./JG 53 and was captured at Sidi Hanesh in November–December 1942 by 7 Squadron SAAF. It still exists in the South Africa War Museum, Johannesburg

Working on getting White 6+I airworthy, Sidi Hanesh, December 1942.

Bf 109 F-4 Trop, Wk Nr 8402 White 8, of Oberleutnant Gustav Rödel's 4./JG 27. This aircraft was recorded as suffering 30 per cent damage at Ain El Gazala on 26 September 1941. The photograph was taken at Gambut in December 1941.

This wreck appears to give few clues. However, just below the cockpit is the Schlageter badge indicating JG 26 and the white markings 7./JG 26. Commanded by Oberleutnant Joachim Müncheberg, 7./JG 26 moved to Ain-el-Gazala on 14 June 1941 and returned to France at the end of September 1941. This photograph was taken at Ain-el-Gazala between December 1941 and February 1942 and the aircraft has obviously been left behind following an accident. The only one this can possibly be is Bf 109 E-7, Wk Nr 6467 which suffered a forced landing resulting in 50 per cent damage on 2 August 1941.

An F-4 Trop minus its spinner carrying out an engine run. The badge on the nose of a shield with a black cross on a white background and three yellow aircraft pointed downwards is the Jesau Kreuz of III./JG 27. It is believed that this aircraft is from Oberleutnant Hans Lass' 8./JG 27, Lass commanding the Staffel from April 1941 to June 1942. Note the white band around the nose.

On 5 May 1943, this Bf 109 G-6, Wk Nr 18046 GP+IZ, of 7./JG 27 suffered engine failure on an armed reconnaissance mission over Malta and force-landed at Luqa. Its pilot, Oberleutnant Günther Hannak, Staffelkapitän of 7./JG 27 since 26 February 1943, was taken prisoner. Hannak joined 2.(Jagd)/LG 2 in February 1941 and shot down his first aircraft, a Blenheim, over Larissa on 15 April 1941. 2.(Jagd)/LG 2 then became 2./JG 77 and he was awarded the Deutsches Kreuz in Gold on 8 June 1942 and the Ritterkreuz on 1 July 1942 by which time he had shot down thirty-eight aircraft. In April 1942, he was given command of the Ölschutzstaffel/JG 77 at Bucharest-Pipera which at the start of August 1942 became 1./JG 4. He was then posted to command 7./JG 27, shooting down two Spitfires on 12 April 1943 taking his score to forty-three (although some records say he had forty-seven). Just under a month later he was captured, having shot down no more aircraft with 7./JG 27. Wk Nr 18046 was a brand-new aircraft and as a result, still carried factory codes as opposed to tactical numerals.

On 31 August 1943, the RAF reported capturing a Bf 109 G-6 Wk Nr 15033 at Elmas/Cagliari. It was described as being marked Yellow 12, had a white band and the undersides of the wingtips were white. The aircraft was also described as being stripped. When the 356th Fighter Squadron/350th Fighter Group USAAF arrived at Elmas on 31 October 1943, this is what they found. Note a second Bf 109 in the background.

By February 1943, the 346th Fighter Squadron had got this aircraft airworthy. Note the 1.(F)/122 badge on the nose. It has been stated that this aircraft was from II./JG 51 whilst the Wk Nr indicates a G-4 Trop not G-6. The Wk Nr was recorded in 1st Lieutenant Hugh D. Dow's logbook; Dow is seen in the cockpit at Elmas.

Completely re-sprayed, the Bf 109's crew chief Sergeant Harold 'Woody' Jenkins decided to rechristen the Bf 109 Red 13; why, Dow does not know, apart from Woody had a 'weird sense of humour'.

Right: 1st Lieutenant Hugh Dow by the nose of 'his' Bf 109 G-4, January 1944.

Below: This Bf 109G-2/R2, Wk Nr 10605 Black 14, of 2.(H)/14 was shot down by Bren gun fire from the Gordon Highlanders and crash-landed at Zarzis, Tunisia, on 20 February 1943. Its pilot, Leutnant Gerhard Wernicke, managed to evade capture and was safe in German hands three days later. Wenicke would be awarded the Ehrenpokal on 12 April 1943 and the Deutsches Kreuz in Gold on 17 October 1943 and would apparently survive the war. This aircraft had the name Irmgard (apparently the name of the girlfriend of Unteroffizier Bopp, Wernicke's first mechanic) on the port side of the fuselage ahead of the cockpit. This aircraft was made airworthy by 79 Fighter Group and was apparently returned to the USA. Note the aerial mast is missing (via Wadman).

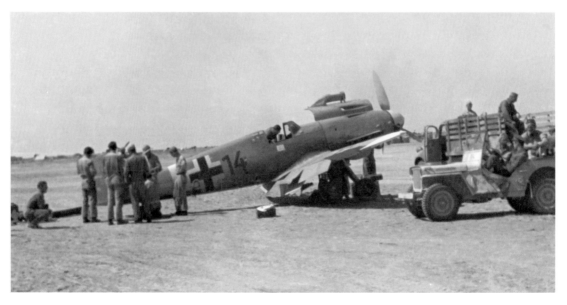

Bf 109 F-4 Trops of III./JG 27 discovered in spring 1942. The nearest is Black 1 of Oberleutnant Hans Lass' 8./JG 27, the next Yellow 5 of 8./JG 27. Behind that is a Stuka of StG 3.

An F-4 Trop Black 11 of Hauptmann Ernst Düllberg's 5./JG 27, Spring 1942. II./JG 27 would continue flying the F-4 until it was replaced by the G-2 Trop towards the end of 1942. Düllberg had taken command of 8./JG 27 in August 1940 and would hand over to Hauptmann Ernst Boerngen on 20 May 1942 by which time his victory score was fifteen. He was then posted to Stab/JG 27 and would be awarded the Ritterkreuz on 27 July 1944 by which time he was commanding III./JG 27. He would survive the war having shot down forty-five aircraft.

Late in 1942, a gathering of aircraft wrecks is seen at El Daba (LG105). Most are F-4 Trops from JG 27 but there are also aircraft from III./JG 53, III./ZG 1 and 4.(H)/12 (the two aircraft with black numbers applied over the rear fuselage bands, namely Black 9 near the middle left edge of the photo and Black 1 at the end of the row of the fuselages which points to 4.(H)/12). The same marking style was previously used by 2.(H)/14 which left Africa in April and came back in November 1942 but during their first tour they flew Bf 109 Es and came back with Bf 109 G-4s. This means that Bf 109 Fs with such markings are from 4.(H)/12. On the right is White 9+- of 4./JG 27 and White 8 of either 4. or 1./JG 27. In the long row on the left is Black 9 of 4.(H)/12, SQ+FT or SQ+ET of an unknown unit, Yellow 6+I of 9./JG 53, White 5+- of 4./JG 27, White 7+- of 4./JG 27, VE+WN of unknown unit, Black< of Stab I./JG 27, White 6 from JG 53 (probably 7 Staffel), Black 1 of 4.(H)/12 and finally a Bf 109 E of III./ZG 1.

Another scrapyard assembled by the Allies in North Africa. The four visible fuselages belong to F-4 Trops White 3+I of 7./JG 53, Yellow 11+I of 9./JG 53, an unidentified JG 53 aircraft with bright single digit marking, and White 10 of Jabogruppe Afrika. There is also a Bf 109 E Black 3 from 2.(H)/14 and Bf 109 F-4 Yellow 2+I of 9./JG 53 but are out of shot. The Bf 110s are an E-2 Wk Nr 2354 3U+DT from 9./ZG 26 (known to have been damaged on 27 June 1942 on a belly-landing at Sidi Barani) and probably another E, in tropical camouflage. Finally the Stuka coded S7+J? might have belonged to 3., 6. or 9./StG. 3.

What appears to be an ERLA-manufactured F-4 Trop of 5./JG 27 which would have had a black numeral and a red bar. Irritatingly, the hat obscures the Wk Nr. (via Rayner)

This Bf 109 G-4 Trop Black 13 of 2.(H)/14 is seen at Safi, Malta in April 1945. Captured at Gerbini by 1 Squadron SAAF, it was eventually flown to Malta where no doubt shortly afterwards it was scrapped.

Obviously F-4 Trops seen in southern Italy in 1942, possibly destined for JG 27. The lack of markings after the fuselage cross and the black/red numerals (2, 1 and 3) could mean 2./JG 27

THE EASTERN FRONT

The triangle on the fuselage of this Bf 109 E-7 indicates the unit to be Hauptmann Otto Weiss' II.(S)/ LG 2 and the White C Oberleutnant Bruno Meyer's 5 Staffel. Meyer would be awarded the Ritterkreuz on 21 August 1941 and survived the war. The aircraft show here is believed to have been flown by Unteroffizier Willi Tritsch who would also be awarded the Ritterkreuz on 23 December 1942 and would also survive the war.

This Bf 109 F-2 <+- of Stab II/JG 3 has force-landed in Russia in the early stages of Operation Barbarossa. Damage is slight so it has not been possible to identify the particular aircraft or its pilot with any degree of certainty. (via Oliver)

The chevron indicates this aircraft was flown by the Gruppen Adjutant and the pilot, an Oberleutnant, stands behind. This is believed to be Oberleutnant Franz Beyer (posted to command 8./JG 3 on 11 July 1941) who is speaking to Oberleutnant Karl Faust (posted to command 4./JG 3 on 27 June 1941 and killed in action on 12 July 1941). Beyer would be awarded the Ritterkreuz on 30 August 1941 and would be killed on 11 February 1944 whilst commanding IV./JG 3 when during combat his Bf 109 G-6, Wk Nr 411036 hit trees between Wéris and Erezée south of Liège in Belgium. He was credited with around eighty-one victories at the time of his death. (via Oliver)

The Bf 109 F-2 clearly showing the <+- markings and the II./JG 3 shield. (via Oliver).

A tripod is in place to lift the aircraft back onto its undercarriage. Damage is slight. (via Oliver)

On 21 September 1941, this Bf 109 F-4, Wk Nr 7073 Yellow 1, of 9./JG 77 collided with a Soviet I-16 and crash-landed at Melitpol. The pilot, Staffelkapitän Oberleutnant Kurt Lasse, was uninjured but the aircraft was written off.

The rudder of Oberleutnant Kurt Lasse's Yellow 1, 21 September 1941. Lasse began the war flying with 6./Jagdgruppe186 (Träger) but moved to 9./JG 77 at the start of July 1940. His first victory was a Blenheim on 18 April 1941 (which is the Greek badge top row far right) and the following day he took command of 9 Staffel following the death in action of Oberleutnant Armin Schmidt. His next victory came on 22 June 1941 and by the time this photograph was taken, his score stood at thirty-one although he was credited with another two victories on 21 September 1941. He would be killed in action on 8 October 1941 when his Bf 109 F-4, Wk Nr 8475 Yellow 1, collided with a MiG-3. His final score was thirty-nine and he would be awarded the Ritterkreuz posthumously on 3 May 1942.

Another view of Wk Nr 7072 on 21 September 1941. There is damage to the top of the cowling and the aircraft is liberally covered with oil and what also appears to be coolant.

Yellow nose and spinner of this Bf 109 F and the tip of a Stab chevron. The unit is possibly JG 3 or JG 54 but there are no other clues.

Opposite: Seen here is Oberleutnant Kurt Quaet Faslem who flew with Stab III./JG 53 from October 1940, getting his first victory over the Soviet Union (his second of the war) on 22 June 1941. He then moved to I./JG 53 in July 1941, his last victory with III Gruppe being his fourth on 26 June 1941. His first victory with I Gruppe came on 25 July 1941, I Gruppe moving west again in August 1941 after which he took command of 2./JG 53 from Hauptmann Ignaz Prestelle on 20 November 1941 when Prestelle took over I./JG 2. He remained with 2./JG 53 flying in Holland (getting one victory on 24 October 1941) before I./JG 53 moved to the Mediterranean in December 1941. In May 1942, I./JG 53 moved back to the Eastern Front but in August 1942 Quaet Faslem was posted to command I./JG 3 by which time he had forty-one victories. He would be killed in an accident on 30 January 1944 flying Bf 109 G-6, Wk Nr 15243 Black 1, which crashed in bad weather at Langeleben. By this time he had been promoted to Major, and had received the Deutsches Kreuz in Gold on 16 November 1942 and the Ehrenpokal on 21 September 1942. He would be awarded the Ritterkreuz posthumously on 9 June 1944 and promoted to Oberstleutnant.

A Bf 109 G-2 Yellow 2+- of 6./JG 54 taxies out at a waterlogged grass airstrip in Russia, spring–early summer 1942. The aircraft has the Grünherz badge beneath the cockpit and the Lion of Aspern badge behind the cowling.

A Russian press photograph of the Bf 109 F-2, Wk Nr 8908 Black 1, of 2./JG 54. Flown by Staffelkapitän Oberleutnant Richard Hein, it suffered engine failure on an operational flight and force-landed 10km west of Kingisepp and the pilot was captured. Hein had taken command of 2 Staffel on 21 June 1941 and shot down his first aircraft three days later. His third and last victory came on 31 July 1941.

Leutnant Heinrich von Schwerdtner in his Bf 109 F-2 Red 4 of 2./JG 53. He shot down his first aircraft on 27 June 1941 which is believed what this photograph shows. By the time I./JG 53 moved west in August 1941, his score had risen to five. His sixth and last victory was a Hurricane on 22 December 1941. On 7 February 1942, he was flying a Bf 109 F-4, Wk Nr 7298 Black 12, which collided landing at Gela with Bf 109 F-4, Wk Nr 7262 Black 3, flown by Leutnant Erich Thomas. Thomas survived but Schwerdtner was killed.

A Bf 109 G of an unidentified unit beats up a Finnish airfield, 1944.

The Bf 109 G-3, Wk Nr 15909 <<5, of II./JG 52 Karlovka, 8 September 1943. This aircraft was flown by Kommandeur Hauptmann Gerhard Barkhorn whose total number of victories would be 301. When this photograph was taken, his score stood at 169 but would increase by another three on this date. Below the cockpit is the name of his wife Christl whilst the number 5 was in white inside the second chevron. Barkhorn would receive the Schwerter on 2 March 1944 and would survive the war. Sadly he and his wife were involved in a car accident on 8 January 1983, Christl dying at the scene and Gerhard passing away two days later.

Hauptmann Franz von Werra took command of I./JG 53 in July 1941. He had recently returned from escaping captivity in Canada and replaced Oberleutnant Wilfried Balfanz who had been reported missing on 24 June 1941. Von Werra's first victory with his new unit was his sixth of the war on 7 July 1941, the previous five being with II./JG 3 in the Battle of Britain. By the time I./JG 53 moved west in August 1941, his score stood at sixteen. Awarded the Ritterkreuz on 14 December 1940, he would be killed on 25 October 1941 when his Bf 109 F-4, Wk Nr 7285, suffered engine failure and crashed in the sea off Vlissingen.

A Bf 109 E-7 of II.(S)/LG 2. The Mickey Mouse badge, adopted by a previous Staffelkapitän Adolf Galland, on the yellow cowling identifies the unit as 4 Staffel which was commanded by Oberleutnant Alfred Druschel in 1941. 4.(S)/LG 2 would become 1./SG 1 in January 1942 and would use the same Mickey Mouse badge. Druschel, a successful ground-attack pilot, would be awarded the Schwerter but would be reported missing in action commanding SG 4 on 1 January 1945 during Operation Bodenplatte, the massed fighter attack on Allied airfields in Belgium and Holland.

Loading four 50kg bombs aboard a Bf 10G-2 of I./JG 54, Krasnowardeisk. I./JG 54 was based at this location off and on from the end of October 1942 to February 1943 when it moved back to Germany.

A well-known photograph, sometimes in colour, of a Bf 109 F-2 of III./JG 53. The photograph is said to have been taken at Konotop which was III./JG 53's home from mid-September to the start of October 1941 when it moved back to Germany in preparation for moving to the Mediterranean. It is therefore possible that this was an aircraft left behind. III./JG 53 was commanded by Hauptmann Wolf-Dietrich Wilcke who had taken command of the Gruppe on 13 August 1940 having previously commanded 7./JG 53

A Bf 109 F, believed to be from JG 5, being worked on in extreme conditions, northern Norway. Unfortunately there are no clues as to the unit, date or precise location.

Feldwebel Heinz Furth and Oberfeldwebel Johann Pichler beside a G-2/R6 Kanonenboot of 7./JG 77.
Pichler joined 7./JG 77 in the summer of 1940, getting his first victory over Crete on 16 May 1941. By
the end of 1941 his score stood at seventeen. He would be shot down and wounded over Italy on 14
July 1943 flying Bf 109 G-6, Wk Nr 18151 White 3, by which time his score stood at thirty-five. He would
be shot down again on 28 July 1944 flying Bf 109 G-6, Wk Nr 265685 White 13, and would be captured
by Soviet troops whilst in hospital. His final score was fifty-two and he was awarded the Ritterkreuz on
19 August 1944. Note the III./JG 77 wolf's head badge.

Bf 109 F-4s of 7./JG 77, Crimea, spring 1942. The aircraft are numbered White 9, 1, 9 and 4.

A closer view of White 6 of 7./JG 77, Crimea, spring 1942. The pilot is reputed to be Oberfeldwebel Johann Pichler but the victory bars on the rudder would not support that this is his regular aircraft as he started 1942 with seventeen victories.

Hastily-applied winter camouflage and the only markings are a White 2. This is a Bf 109 G-6 of 10./JG 54 captured by the Soviets, January 1944.

Another captured aircraft was this Bf 109 G-4/R6, Wk Nr 14997 KJ+GU White 2, of 7./JG 52. Unteroffizier Herbert Meissler suffered engine failure after combat near Taman on 28 May 1943 and he force-landed to be captured. This aircraft was previously flown by Oberleutnant Erich Hartmann of 9./JG 52 who would go on to shoot down 352 aircraft and be awarded the Brillanten.

Bf 109 G-2 Yellow 1 of 3./JG 4 at Mizil, Romania. This Gruppe was formed one Staffel at a time with 3 Staffel apparently not being formed until January 1943. The pilot is believed to be Oberleutnant Manfred Spenner formerly of 3./JG 52 and I and III./JG 53 who became Staffelkapitän of 3./JG 4. He would be shot down by Flak 3km south of Statione di Carraota and taken prisoner on 9 March 1944 flying Bf 109 G-6, Wk Nr 161371 Yellow 3.

A Bf 109 G-2 of II./JG 5 about to taxi out at either Idriza, Dno or Dorpat, 1943–4, to escort Stukas of either I./SG 5 or SG 3. The badge on the nose is II./JG 5's four-leafed clover in a diamond.

A spectacular accident to a Bf 109 F-4, Black 2 of 8./JG 77, summer 1941. With the three victory bars on the rudder, it has been suggested this is the aircraft of Oberfeldwebel Friedrich Blaurock who had three claims between 4 July and 17 August 1941 but he was with 7./JG 77, being shot down on 25 July 1941 flying Bf 109 E-4, Wk Nr 2012 Yellow 5, but managing to evade capture. He would be killed in an accident flying at Bü 131 of 2./Jagdlehrer-Uberprüfungsgruppe on 18 April 1944.

Crimea, April–May 1942. To the left is mechanic Obergefreiter Gerhard Bohl and to the right Feldwebel Alfred Grislawski. Grislawski joined 9./JG 52 in November 1940 but did not shoot down his first aircraft until 1 September 1941 and by the end of 1941 had been credited with eleven aircraft. This would increase to eighty-four at the end of 1942, having been awarded the Ritterkreuz on 1 July 1942 by which time he was with 7./JG 52. He would be injured in an explosion of a German landmine on 4 June 1943 with his score standing at 109. After recuperation, he was posted to 1./JGr Süd, then Stab./JG 50 and 1./JG 1 as Staffelkapitän. By the end of 1943, his score stood at 119 and in March 1944 he took command of 8./JG 1 and in September 1944, 11./JG 53. He would be shot down on 26 September 1944 flying a Bf 109 G-14, Wk Nr 462649 Black 6, after having shot down a P-38 for his 133rd victory. His parachute only opened just before he hit the ground and the subsequent injuries meant he never flew again. He would be awarded the Eichenlaub on 11 April 1944.

Oberleutnant Erich Hartmann's Bf 109 G-6 Yellow 1 of 9./JG 52, Novosaporovyi/ Nowo-Zaporoshye, 2 October 1943. On this day, Hartmann got his 121st victory, a LaGG-5. Just visible below the cockpit is the pierced red heart of the Karaya Staffel.

A Bf 109 F-2 Black 6 of 5./JG 52. The scoreboard for 5./JG 52 (formerly 2./JG 52's badge) of a red devil with a bow and arrow is in the foreground showing seventeen victories in the West and seventy-three in the East, the 73rd coming on 30 November, one of two victories to Oberleutnant Siegfried Simsch, the Staffelkapitän, his 23rd and 24th of the war. Simsch had been with 5./JG 52 since early 1940, getting his first victory on 14 February 1941. He was awarded the Ritterkreuz on 1 July 1941 but would be killed in action over Normandy commanding I./JG 11 on 8 June 1944, his final score believed to be fifty-four.

Bf 109 G-2s of 1./JG 4, Mizil, Romania, summer 1943. The furthest aircraft is coded White 2. Commanded by Hauptmann Franz Hahn, Mizil was this Gruppe's base from its formation in August 1942 until 26 November 1943 when it moved to Germany. Hahn, an experienced pre-war fighter pilot, was killed in action 22 January 1944 when he hit the tail baling out of his Bf 109 G-6 which then crashed 2km south-east of Littorio airfield. He was awarded the Deutsches Kreuz in Gold posthumously.

Bf 109 F-4 White <+I of Stab III./JG 54, Siwerskaja, June–July 1942. The pilot is the Adjutant of III./
JG 54, Leutnant Erwin Leykauf, whose aircraft sports the Arms of Ansbach, the place of his birth, in
addition to the JG 54 green heart. Leykauf was a very experienced fighter pilot, flying as an NCO with
2./JG 21, then 8./JG 54. He was shot down on 6 July 1941, force-landed on 30 March 1942 and then
shot down and wounded on 29 September 1942 after which he was posted to command 12./JG 26. He
then returned to JG 54, then JG 2 and ended the war with JG 7. He was awarded the Deutsches Kreuz
in Gold 4 August 1942 and was credited with eight night and twenty-five day victories.

This photograph gives away little apart from it is a Bf 109 F-4 which has force-landed in Russia.

A clue is given to the previous photo by the II./JG 3 shield.

It has been suggested that this aircraft is Wk Nr 7095 which crashed on take-off on 26 August 1942 at Stschastlijwa, injuring Unteroffizier Kuno Bälz. However, it is believed in fact to be Wk Nr 7615 which suffered Flak damage and force-landed at Ossinowka on 18 August 1942. Just visible in this photograph is the Stab chevron

FOREIGN

Major Eino Luukkanen, commanding officer of LeLv 34, walking away from Bf 109 G-2, Wk Nr 14726 MT-203 formerly RF+UV, Utti, 24 April 1943. This aircraft would become the first G-2 to be lost when it crashed on 20 May 1943. Luukkanen (4 June 1909–9 April 1964) was Finland's third highest-scoring ace credited with fifty-six victories.

This Messerschmitt AG Augsburg Press photograph is described as Finnish pilots collecting their Bf 109 G-2s at Erding, early 1943. In fact it shows pilots of 1/LeLv 24 at Utti on 2 June 1943. Left to right: Captain Pauli Ervi, Lieutenant Väinö Pokela, Warrant Officer Mauno Fräntilä, Chief Warrant Officer Oiva Tuominen, Lieutenant Kalevi Tervo, Sergeant Gösta Lönnfors and Sergeant Urho Lehto. In the background is Bf 109 G-2, Wk Nr 14753 MT-212 formerly RJ+SW, the personal aircraft of Chief Warrant Officer Eino Juutilainen (21 February 1914–21 February 1999), Finland's top-scoring fighter pilot with 94½th victories.

An accident between two Hungarian Bf 109 G-14s coded V8-72 and W1-43. Latter was Wk Nr 511221 and served with 101/6 vadászszázad based at Vezprém, Hungary, in late 1944.

A Bf 109 G-2 White 7 of Grupul 7, Esc No 53 at Bucharest-Otopeni, 1944. The badge on the nose is Mickey Mouse on a charger. The underneath of the nose, wingtips and fuselage band are yellow whilst the rudders are white.

Capitan Manuel Bengoechea Menchaca of 2a Escuadrilla Azul or 15 (Span)./JG51 seen at Orel in 1942 with a Bf 109 F-2. After training at JFS 1 from March until June 1942, he and his unit arrived at Orel and commenced operations from 26 June 1942. His first kill came on 5 July 1942, his fifth and last on 29 October 1942.

Hard to spot but this aircraft's nationality is given away by the uniforms. A Hungarian MWG Györ-built Bf 109 G-6 of 101 vadászszázad based at Vezprém, Spring 1944. The Wk Nr would start with 760. This unit is identified as either as 101. vadászrepülő-osztály (101. Fighter Group), or 101. vadászezred (101. Fighter Wing), depending on the time when the photos were taken: the Group was created on 1 May 1944 from three squadrons and based at Veszprém-Jutas airfield where it remained until spring 1945. In September 1944 the Group was expanded to a Wing, consisting of two Groups (three squadrons each – the sixth becoming a training unit). The first Group remained at Veszprém whilst the second was formed at Kenyeri.

CAPTURED

Still carrying its German marking is this Bf 109 F-4/B, Wk Nr 7232 formerly White 11, of 10./JG 26. It was hit by machine-gun fire while attacking a ship off Newhaven on 20 May 1942 and crash-landed at Beachy Head, Unteroffizier Oswald Fischer being captured. The aircraft had been hit in the engine and was taken to the RAE then to 1426 (Enemy Aircraft) Flt where it received a new engine. Painted in RAF colours, it was allocated the serial number NN644. It was damaged in an accident on 7 January 1944 and after being put into storage, was scrapped after the war.

This view of Wk Nr 7232/NN644 appears to show damage to the port wingtip. It suffered damage to the port wing and aileron when it ground-looped at Thurleigh on 7 January 1944.

Confusion exists as to the identity of this Bf 109 G-6/Trop. It was captured in the Mediterranean in 1943 and was thought to have served with I./JG 77. It is now thought that it was possibly Wk Nr 15270 RP+DT Yellow 14 of 6./JG 53 captured at Comiso in July 1943. It was shipped to 1426 (EAC) Flt at RAF Collyweston arriving in February 1944 where the underwing gun pods and tropical filter were removed and it was allocated the serial VX101. Confusion still exists as to its fate, either being damaged in a landing accident at RAF Thorney Island on 19 May or 26 September 1944, after which it was used for spares.

This Bf 109 G-2/U2, Wk Nr 412951 NS+FE coded White 16, of 1./JG 301 was captured when it landed at RAF Manston at 0240hrs on 21 July 1944. Its pilot, Leutnant Horst Prenzel, became lost on a night fighter mission over France. Five minutes later another Bf 109 G-6, Wk Nr 163240 RQ+BD Yellow 8, of 3./JG 301 flown by Feldwebel Manfred Gromill did the same thing, although this pilot retracted the undercarriage after touching down.

In addition to a jettisonable fuel tank, the aircraft had a 20mm MG 151/20 firing through the propeller hub, two MG 151/20s in underwing gondolas and two 13mm MG 131s on top of the engine.

Wk Nr 412951 was described as being camouflaged grey all over with khaki and blue mottling on the upper surfaces. The spinner had a white and black spiral and the fuselage band was brown.

Wk Nr 412951 became TP814 and was delivered to the Air Fighting Development Unit at RAF Wittering on 31 August 1944 where it was used for trials, flying against Spitfire LF.IVs and XIVs and a Mustang III.

TP814's RAF career was short-lived as on 23 November 1944 it suffered an accident taking off from RAF Wittering, which this photograph shows.

With non-standard camouflage, serial RN228 identifies this aircraft as Bf 109 G-2, Wk Nr 10639 PG+QJ Black 6, of 8./JG 77. Flown by Leutnant Heinz Lüdemann, it was damaged in combat and force-landed near Gambut on either 4 or 7 November 1942 only for it to be captured intact four days later. It was apparently not Lüdemann's aircraft but that of Feldwebel Eduard Isken. Lüdemann had force-landed Bf 109 G-2 Wk Nr 10472 near Mga on the Eastern Front on 25 September 1943 and would be killed in action flying a Black 1, Bf 109 G-2 Wk Nr 10819, north of Ksar Rhilane, Tunisia, on 10 March 1943, shot down by Pilot Officer Rae Guess of 112 Squadron by which time his score stood at five aircraft shot down in combat. Wk Nr 10639 was shipped to the UK, apparently not arriving at 1426 (Enemy Aircraft) Flight at RAF Collyweston until 26 December 1943 where it was reassembled and first flown on 19 February 1944. It then flew trials against other Allied fighters before going into storage in November 1945. It was later restored to flying condition only for it to be damaged in an accident in October 1997 and is now on display at RAF Cosford.

The markings on this Bf 109 G-4 are not Luftwaffe ones, nor are the two personnel on the wing German and the aircraft in the background has a Soviet star. It is believed that this is one of three aircraft from 13 (Slovak)./JG 52 which deserted to the Soviets in September 1943. On 9 September 1943, Unterfeldwebel Anton Matŭsek in Wk Nr 19347 Yellow 9 and Unteroffizier Ludovit Dobrovedski in Wk Nr 16269 Yellow 13 were tasked with escorting a Fw 189 but instead of returning to base, presumed to be Anapa, they landed at Novomalorssiyskaya. Two days later Unteroffizier Alexandr Gierić did the same in Wk Nr 14938 Yellow 2.

Seen at RAF Wittering on 19 October 1949 is this Bf 109 G-14 Wk Nr 464863. Only a handful, if any, G-14s saw operational service. (via Gomersall)

Wk Nr 464863 was captured by British troops at Eggebek in Denmark. It had the Wk Nr stencilled on the tail and a black-and-white spiral spinner. Its unit is not known (although JG 102 was still based there at the end of the war) and no doubt it was scrapped shortly afterwards. (via Gomersall)